MILITARY
ILLUSTRATED
MARINE
U.S. MARINE CORPS HEROES OF THE PACIFIC WAR
WRITTEN BY RON FIELD

COLOUR PLATES BY RICHARD HOOK

SERIES EDITOR TIM NEWARK

Current titles
Marine
Stormtrooper
Rifleman
Highlander

Future titles
Ranger
Paratrooper
Legionary
Samurai

Dedication
For Harry Daniels Reeks, Combat Artist, USMC
– Semper Fidelis!

First published in 1999 in Great Britain
by Publishing News Ltd

UK editorial office:
Military Illustrated, 39 Store Street,
London WC1E 7DB, Great Britain

Ron Field has asserted his moral right to be
identified as the author of this work.

ISBN 1-903040-00-0

Designed by Atelier Works

Printed and bound in Singapore under
the supervision of M.R.M. Graphics Ltd,
Winslow, Buckinghamshire

CONTENTS

BIRTH OF THE MARINE

On 28 February 1945, a patrol from the 28th Marines reached the summit of Mount Suribachi and raised a small American flag to announce the success of the United States landings on the southern tip of Iwo Jima, in the Volcano Islands. Witnessing the incident through his binoculars, Secretary of the Navy James Forrestal turned to Major General Holland M. Smith, United States Marine Corps, commander of the Amphibious Corps Pacific Fleet, and announced: 'The raising of that flag on Suribachi means there will be a Marine Corps for the next 500 years'. Possibly realising the historical significance of the occasion, a Marine officer sent for a larger flag and acquired one from Landing Ship Tank 779. The second flag-raising was captured in a still photograph taken by Associated Press photographer Joe Rosenthal, and complemented Forrestal's sense of history. The haunting image of six ordinary young Americans, three of whom were killed and two wounded during the remaining fighting on the island, has come to symbolise the US Marine Corps of World War Two.

The use of sea soldiers, or 'marines', is as ancient as war at sea. When the Persians invaded Athens in 480 BC, Themistocles mobilised his sea power and decreed that twenty *epibatae*, or heavily-armed soldiers, should serve aboard each trireme. In the 2nd century BC, *milites classiarii*, or 'soldiers of the fleet', were specially trained and armed for duty aboard Roman quinqueremes, one legion being attached to each fleet. Although ordinary foot soldiers were often crammed aboard warships in the Middle Ages, it was not until the 16th century that the unique role of the marine was re-discovered when the Spanish *Infanteria del Armada* was founded in 1537. As further recognition of the need for 'naval infantry', Cardinal Armand Jean du Plessis Richelieu authorised the *Compagnie de la Mer*, or 'Company of the Sea', in 1622. Composed of French sailors trained to go ashore as infantrymen, this unit later developed into the *1e Régiment de Marine*. The next corps of

marines, or soldiers trained to serve aboard ship, was organised during the Dutch Wars between Britain and Holland. On 28 October 1664, Charles II decreed the formation of the 'The Duke of York and Albany's Maritime Regiment of Foot', or 'Lord High Admiral's Regiment'. Disbanded after the Glorious Revolution of 1688, this unit was soon replaced by the 1st and 2nd Regiments of Marines, still later becoming the Royal Marines. Meanwhile on 10 December 1665 the *Regiment de Marine* had been organised in Holland by Admiral Michiel de Ruyter and Secretary of State, Jan de Witt.

FIRST AMERICAN MARINES

The first sea soldiers in the New World were raised in the American colonies in 1740. The 3,000 marines organised to fight against the Spaniards that year wore 'camlet coats, brown linen waistcoats, and canvas trousers', and largely consisted of impressed men who were debtors, criminals, and vagrants. Commanded by amateur officers eager to gain a Crown commission, they were originally led by Colonel Alexander Spottswood of Virginia, who died soon after taking command. Hence the unit became known as 'Gooch's Marines' after another Virginian, William Gooch, who led them into action when the British attacked the Spanish naval base at Cartagena in northern Colombia during April 1741. Landing unopposed in Cuba during the following July, they secured Guantanamo Bay as a base for the British fleet. One of Gooch's Marine officers at this time was Captain Lawrence Washington, half-brother of George Washington, the future President of the United States!

Despite their rough edges, the service of colonial units such as Gooch's Marines in the Royal Navy forged valuable links between American and British marines. Although they became enemies during the Revolutionary War and the War of 1812, they later served shoulder to shoulder in Samoa, the Boxer Rebellion, both World Wars, Korea, and the Gulf War.

Common traditions are still shared today. Both services wear full dress blues faced with scarlet and gold. The Royal Marines wear a 'globe and laurel' device displaying the Eastern Hemisphere, while the United States Marine Corps eventually adopted an 'eagle, globe and anchor' device, or 'chicken on a ball', showing the Western Hemisphere.

At the beginning of the Revolutionary War in 1775, seven of the original thirteen American colonies organised their own Marine force to serve aboard ships of their embryonic navies. The Pennsylvania State Marines wore a brown coat with green lapels and turnbacks, and pewter buttons bearing the inscription '1 P B', possibly indicating the unit designation 'First Pennsylvania Battalion of Marines'. The uniform of the Maryland State Marines was a 'blue hunting shirt'. The first truly American Marines were organised later the same year. Meeting in Philadelphia on 10 November, the Second Continental Congress passed a resolution establishing 'the first & second battalions of American Marines' to serve 'for and during the present war between Great Britain and the colonies'. Sponsored by John Adams, this established the Continental Marines and marked the birth date of the United States Marine Corps. Two weeks later, Samuel Nicholas, a blacksmith's

One of the earliest flag raisings of the Continental Marines, painted by Colonel Charles H. Waterhouse, USMC Retired. About midnight on 27 January 1778, twenty-six Marines under Captain John Trevett landed at New Providence in the British-held Bahamas and captured Fort Nassau. At dawn the next day, Trevett had the Stars and Stripes hoisted over the battlements of the decaying fort. *US Marine Corps Art Collection*

son, was commissioned the first Marine officer. Nicholas remained the senior Marine officer throughout the American Revolution and is considered to be the first Marine Commandant. The recruits gathered at the Tun Tavern, a hostelry on the east side of King Street, Philadelphia, in 1775, were required to be 'good seamen, or so acquainted with maritime affairs as to be able to serve to advantage by sea.'

The first American Marines distinguished themselves in a number of important operations. On 3 March 1776, Captain Nicholas led 268 men ashore in a raid on two stone forts on New Providence Island, in the British-held Bahamas, to secure much needed gunpowder for the Continental Army. Capturing only 24 barrels of powder, the Marines also managed to haul off 88 guns, 15 mortars, plus 16,535 shells and balls! On its homeward voyage, the small American fleet exchanged shots with the British corvette *Glasgow*, and one Marine officer and six enlisted men were killed, while four more were wounded. The Marines had been blooded! Arriving back in an American port, Nicholas received the congratulations of John Hancock, President of the Continental Congress, and George Washington paid his respects to the whole fleet.

Rewarded with a major's commission on 25 June 1776, Nicholas continued to recruit four companies of Marines for the Continental Navy frigates then being built in Philadelphia. During the following September, Congress stipulated the uniform of the Marine officer which was 'A green coat faced with white, round cuff, slashed sleeves and pockets, with buttons round the cuff, silver epaulette on the right shoulder, skirts turned back, buttons to suit the facings; white waistcoat and breeches edged with green, black gaiters and garters...' A requisition for uniforms for enlisted men serving on the *Boston*, found in the manuscript diary of Lieutenant of Marines William Jennison, dated 11 April 1778, requested '40 green coats faced with white, 40 white waistcoats, 40 white breeches, the buttons for the whole to be plain white'. According to a description published in the *Pennsylvania Gazette and Weekly Advertiser*, the 'regimentals' of enlisted men by 1779 consisted of a 'green coat with red facings, white woolen jacket, light colored cloth breeches, woolen stockings, and a round hat with white binding'. Reasons for the change from white to red facings are not known. Enlisted men were also to wear green shirts 'if and when they could be procured'.

As the Board of Admiralty had stipulated that a major of Marines should serve at sea on a ship-of-the-line, which the US at that time did not possess,

Nicholas was forced to remain land bound, often behind a desk, for the remainder of the war. Nonetheless, he did participate in several important battles alongside the Continental Army. Three hundred Marines under his command were attached to the Pennsylvania militia division and played a vital role in the withdrawal from Assunpink Creek during the second Battle of Trenton on 2 January 1777. The next day, Nicholas' unit participated in Washington's victory at Princeton. Following this success, the Marines shared the icy fortunes of the Continental Army in winter camp at Morristown, New Jersey, after which they reported back to Philadelphia for further duty.

Onboard ship, Marine detachments served much further afield. The two raids on British soil conducted by Marines from John Paul Jones' sloop-of-war *Ranger* in April 1778, rate among only a handful of successful hostile landings in Britain since 1066. The first raid took place at Whitehaven, in the Solway Firth, during which the guns of two coastal batteries were spiked. Sailing across the Firth, they next landed at St. Mary's Isle, hoping to take the Earl of Selkirk as a hostage to be traded for American prisoners. Learning of their approach, the Earl made his escape, and the raiders contented themselves with carrying off the family silver! The Countess of Selkirk later recalled the

John Adams, American Commissioner to France in 1779, reviews the *Infanterie Irlandaise, Regiment de Walsh-Serrant*, who had volunteered as Marines on board the American ship *Bonhomme Richard*, commanded by John Paul Jones. Painting by Colonel Charles H. Waterhouse, USMC Retired. US Marine Corps Art Collection

'vile blackguard look' of one of the American naval officers present, but remarked on the good behaviour of 'a civil young man in a green uniform, an anchor on his buttons.. [who] seemed naturally well bred'. Alas, Marine Lieutenant Samuel Wallingford was the only American killed when the *Ranger* exchanged shots with HMS *Drake* 24 hours later. Captain Jones subsequently wrote to the Countess from France promising the return of her silver.

The Marines serving aboard the *Bonhomme Richard*, another vessel under Jones' command, consisted of a detachment of the *Infanterie Irlandaise, Regiment de Walsh-Serrant,* on loan from Louis XVI of France. Dressed in red coats with blue facings, and commanded by Irish officers, these men played a vital role as sharpshooters during Jones' victory over HMS *Serapis* in the battle of Flamborough Head off the east coast of England on 23 September 1779.

Back in North America, Marines under Captain John Welsh were involved in an abortive attempt to capture a British fort at Penobscot Bay in Maine during July 1779. A force of 1200 men, including 300 Marines, conducted an amphibious assault and scaled a 200-foot high cliff, driving off the defending Highlanders. The failure of the US Navy commander to provide further support, plus the arrival of a British squadron which drove off the American vessels, left the Marines and some militia stranded on the coast. Retiring southward, most of the sea soldiers found their way back to Boston on foot through the Maine wilderness.

Further west, Captain James Willing led a 34-man company of Marines drawn from the hardened soldiers then stationed at Fort Pitt, down the Mississippi River on an old riverboat converted into an armed vessel and re-named the *Rattletrap,* to harass pro-British plantations and settlements around Natchez. Setting off on 10 January 1778, they succeeded in their mission, capturing slaves, provisions, and plate, and burning much property. After the departure back east of Willing, this same unit, led by Lieutenant Robert George, fought under General George Rogers Clark against the Indians near Lake Michigan in the Illinois territory.

The Treaty of Paris in April 1783 brought an end to the Revolutionary War. At the height of the struggle, the Marines numbered 124 officers and about 3000 men. As the last of the Navy's ships were sold, the Continental Navy and Marines went out of existence. According to an old service tale, the Army and Navy took an inventory at the end of the war and found some mules and a company of Marines surplus to requirements. Flipping a coin, the Army won and took the mules!

Oil painting of Samuel Nicholas, of Philadelphia, who was commissioned a captain on 28 November 1775, and charged with raising the Marines provided for by Congress. A blacksmith's son and inn keeper, he remained senior officer in the Continental Marines throughout the Revolution, and is considered to be the first Marine Commandant. *Defense Department Photo (Marine Corps) 523395*

LEATHERNECKS

During the ten years which followed, the young American nation was defenceless against foreign aggression as the Royal Navy, French privateers, and Algerian corsairs played havoc amongst its merchant shipping. In 1794, Congress finally reactivated the Navy with the passage of an Act providing for the construction of six frigates, and the recruitment of an adequate number of seamen and Marines to man them. But it was not until 11 July 1798 that the latter was formally established, and the United States Marine Corps was born. The Corps of 1798 was to consist of 33 officers and 848 'noncommissioned officers, musicians, and privates'. Within 24 hours of its establishment, President John Adams had appointed William Ward Burrows, of Charleston, South Carolina, as Major Commandant of the Corps.

As an economy measure, the new Corps was provided with blue uniforms faced with red which were left over from the Revolutionary War, as worn by the Rifle Battalions of the Legion. Thus began the first use of the now familiar Marine 'dress blues'. According to a description recorded on 26 October 1798, enlisted men wore a 'Blue cloth jacket, lapelled and faced with red, edged with red and a red belt'. Underneath this was a 'Red vest, [and] blue woolen overalls with red seams'. All these garments were fastened by 'naval buttons' bearing 'an Eagle, with a shield on the left wing, enclosing a foul anchor'. Headgear consisted of 'A common hat, trimmed with yellow, turned up on the left side with a leather cockade'. White linen 'overalls' were supplied for summer wear. All enlisted men also wore high, stiff leather collars, or stocks, to keep heads erect, which inspired the Marine Corps nickname 'leatherneck'. Original arms consisted of either French 'Charleville' muskets or new Springfields. In time these were replaced where possible by shorter 'Tower' muskets, which were easier to handle in rigging by ships' detachments.

The role of the new corps was to be 'of amphibious nature', with particular responsibility for the enforcement of shipboard discipline. Additional responsibilities included 'duty in the forts and garrisons of the United States', plus 'any other duty on shore, as the President, at his discretion shall direct'. Originally set up in Philadelphia, Marine Headquarters was moved to a site near the Navy Yard in the new Federal capital at Washington during June 1800. Marines were to be immune from arrest for debt and, like their British counterparts, were governed by the 'Articles of War' while ashore, and by the Navy Regulations when afloat!

The earliest action seen by the fledgling

US Marine Corps was against the French Navy. Since the deterioration of relationships between the two nations in 1794, French privateers had been seizing American merchant shipping and impressing their seamen. Finally in 1798, President Adams acknowledged that his country was engaged in an 'undeclared naval war'. Following a series of victorious single-ship actions by the small but spirited US Navy, the new Marine Corps conducted its first landing on a foreign shore. On 12 May 1800, Marines detailed to the frigate *Constitution*, and commanded by Captain Daniel Carmick, took part in a raid on French shipping at Puerto Plata on the north coast of the Spanish island of Santo Domingo. Entering the harbour undetected with his men below decks in a commandeered coaster, Carmick later recalled that the operation reminded him of 'the wooden horse of Troy'. Drawing quietly alongside the *Sandwich,* a captured British ship held in the harbour by the French, the Marines rushed onboard yelling like 'devils' and took her crew completely by surprise. Carmick's command next waded ashore to storm Fortaleza San Felipe and spike its guns before making good their escape in the *Sandwich*. Although acclaimed as a resounding success, the attack proved to be a breach of Spain's nominal neutrality, and the US Navy was required to

On 28 July 1779, 200 Continental Marines under Captain John Welch scrambled out of their ships' boats and climbed the bluff above Penobscot Bay on the Maine coast, in what turned out to be an unsuccessful attempt to force the British out of Fort George. The arrival of a British fleet forced the Americans to retire up the Penobscot River, where

they burned their vessels and retreated southward through the Maine wilderness. This was to be the last amphibious assault conducted by American Marines until the war with Mexico in 1846.
Painting by Colonel Charles H. Waterhouse, USMC Retired. US Marine Corps Art Collection

return the *Sandwich* back to the French!

With the ending of hostilities with France in February 1801, and a need for greater economy, the US Navy faced drastic cut-backs. Consequently, on 21 May 1802, President Thomas Jefferson ordered the Marines reduced to a mere 26 officers and 453 enlisted men.

Three months after peace with France, the US became embroiled in the Barbary Wars in the Mediterranean. For years the threat of Barbary pirates, or corsairs, had been used by Tripoli, Tunis, Morocco, and Algiers to compel the US and the European Powers into paying protection money. By 1801, America was paying a tribute of more than two million dollars a year – a sum more than one fifth of its annual federal revenue. During that year, the Bey of Tripoli, Yusuf Karamanli, demanded more money, and President Jefferson refused to pay. Chopping down the flagpole before the American consulate, the Tripolitan ruler declared war on the US!

Amid the numerous small amphibious landings and ferocious sea-fights, the most outstanding event of this war was the American-led overland campaign against the fortress at Derna. A force of about 350 mercenaries under the putative command of Hamet Karamanli, the Bey of Tripoli's exiled older brother, set out from Alexandria on a 600-mile trek across the Libyan desert during March 1805. Raised and led by US diplomatic agent William H. Eaton, they were accompanied by a squad of seven US Marines under First Lieutenant Presley Neville O'Bannon, who acted as Eaton's personal bodyguard. After re-provisioning and drawing munitions from US navy vessels along the coast, the expedition finally arrived at Derna and assaulted its fortress on 24 April. O'Bannon's Marines, plus the mercenaries, spearheaded the attack while three American warships shelled the city. Among the 14 men who fell during the assault were three Marines, two of whom died. Meanwhile, Lieutenant O'Bannon had the honour of being the first American officer to hoist the Stars and Stripes over a captured citadel in the 'Old World'.

Eaton's force next held Derna against a Tripolitan army until June 1805, when they learned that the US had negotiated a peace treaty with Yusuf Karamanli. Disappointed in their endeavours, the American Marines eventually evacuated the fort, but not before Hamet Karamanli had rewarded Lieutenant O'Bannon with an Arab, or 'Mameluke', scimitar. In 1826, a sword with a Mameluke hilt patterned after O'Bannon's scimitar was introduced for all US Marine officers. Abandoned in 1859 for the heavier naval officer's sword with metal guard and wire-wrapped leather grip, the Mameluke-

pattern was re-introduced in 1875, although Marine non-commissioned officers continued to carry the straight sword. As a further consequence of O'Bannon's success, the Colors carried by the Corps were inscribed with the words: 'To the Shores of Tripoli'.

After ten years of tension and rivalry on the High Seas, the United States went to war again with Great Britain in June 1812. By this time the Marine Corps consisted of a mere 10 officers and 483 enlisted men, while the US Navy had only sixteen ships on its list. Nonetheless, the Marines distinguished themselves on both land and at sea. Writing to a friend after being appointed to command the Marines on board Captain Isaac Hull's frigate *Constitution,* First Lieutenant William Bush declared: 'Should an opportunity be afforded for boarding the enemy, I will be the first man upon his deck.' On 19 August 1812, Bush's wish came true when his ship engaged the British frigate *Guerriére* in the North Atlantic. As the vessels ground together at close quarters, Bush leapt to the taffrail, called out to his captain, 'Shall I board her, Sir?' and was shot dead by a Royal Marine! Undeterred, the Marine marksmen in the *Constitution's* tops swept the British decks and did much to bring about the final surrender of the first British man-of-war since the Revolutionary War. When the news of Bush's death reached Washington, Marine Commandant Lieutenant Colonel Franklin Wharton ordered all officers to wear black crepe on the left arm and sword hilt for one month.

During the epic cruise of the *Essex* against the British whaling fleet in the Pacific, Lieutenant John Marshall Gamble had the honour of being the only Marine officer ever to command a ship. Given charge of a British vessel captured off the Galapagos Islands in April 1813, he gave chase to and subsequently damaged the 22-gun British raider *Seringapatam.* Gamble and a handful of Marines later protected Navy Captain David Porter and his crew from hostile Typee natives, and the young lieutenant eventually survived being wounded and cast adrift in an open boat by mutinous British prisoners.

The finest hour at sea for the Marines of the 1812 War came in defeat. In an action off Boston on 1 June 1813, the frigate *Chesapeake,* commanded by Captain James Lawrence, a friend of Commodore Oliver Hazard Perry, was disabled by the guns of HMS *Shannon.* As the two ships closed, Lawrence was mortally wounded by a musket ball aimed by a lieutenant of the Royal Marines. As he uttered his last words, 'Don't give up the ship! Sink her! Blow her up!', a British boarding party hacked its way on to the *Chesapeake's* quarterdeck to be met by the American Marine guard, under Lieutenant James Broome, who put up a stubborn resistance. Broome was shot dead while his Marines fought valiantly until the last man, losing thirty-four of forty-four men.

Several months later, on 12 August, Commodore Perry's flagship *Lawrence* flew from her masthead a blue battle flag crudely lettered, 'Don't give up the Ship', when he met with a more heavily armed British squadron of six ships on the waters of Lake Erie. During the fight, Perry's Marine officer, Lieutenant John Brook had his hip shot away and bled to death, but the victorious American Commodore was eventually able to report: 'We have met the enemy and they are ours.'

STAR SPANGLED BANNER

In a futile attempt to protect the capital at Washington, a force of seamen serving five guns, and supported by a Marine battalion commanded by Captain Samuel Miller, held back an onslaught of British light infantry during the Battle of Bladensburg in Maryland on 24 August 1814. The final repulse of the British was actually followed up with a counter-attack led by cutlass-wielding sailors and Miller's Marines yelling 'Board 'em! Board 'em!' Shortly after this, a detachment

of Marines under Lieutenant J. L. Kuhn formed part of the garrison defending Fort McHenry and Sparrows Point in Baltimore, an action which inspired a prominent Washington lawyer, Francis Scott Key, to write 'The Star Spangled Banner', which eventually became the official national anthem of the United States in 1931.

During 1814, Congress had authorised that the Marines be increased to forty-seven officers and nearly eight hundred enlisted men, but it was too late to be of use, and the Corps ended the war with little more manpower than it had at the outset of hostilities.

The final British assault on New Orleans in January 1815 actually took place two weeks after the Peace of Ghent ended hostilities. In this action, some of Major Daniel Carmick's fifty-six man company of Marines fought with Plauché's Creole Battalion in a redoubt at the extreme right flank of the American line. Pushed out of their post at one point by the Peninsular War veterans of Wellington's brother-in-law, General Sir Edward Pakenham, they rallied and held their position while the main British assault was crushed with heavy losses by Andrew Jackson's forces further towards the centre.

Although the Marines fought bravely during the 1812-14 war, their record was overshadowed by

'The charge at Derna', painted by Colonel Charles H. Waterhouse, USMC Retired, depicts the moment First Lieutenant Presley N. O'Bannon and his squad of US Marines captured the Tripolitan fortress of Derna on 27 April 1805.
Peter Newark's Military Pictures

scandal. Commandant Franklin Wharton loaded the Marine pay chest in a wagon and fled Washington prior to the British attack. Berated by fellow Marine officers for failure to take the field, he finally faced a court-martial in 1817. Acquitted, he was urged to resign by President James Monroe, but doggedly maintained his post until his death on 1 September 1818. His successor, Major Anthony Gale, was cashiered for drunkenness after only two years in office.

In 1820, Brevet Major Archibald Henderson was appointed the fifth Commandant of the Marines, and a new era began for the Corps. Desiring a wider role for the Marines in shaping the destiny of the United States, he moulded the Corps into a fighting unit, and gave his men an *esprit de corps* that few other elite military organisations have been able to achieve.

During the next twelve years, Marine detachment were involved as the US Navy chased pirates in the Caribbean, and showed the 'Stars and Stripes' everywhere from Sumatra to the Falkland Islands. It was at home, however, that the Corps encountered its next serious enemy. On 8 December 1829, President Andrew Jackson created consternation throughout its ranks by a recommendation to merge the Marines into 'the artillery or infantry', based on the belief that 'no peculiar training' was

Marines of the *Alliance*, the last Continental frigate in active service, gather ashore on 1 April 1783 for their final pay before being mustered out. Under the watchful eye of Lieutenant Thomas Elwood, they were paid in coin and given a certificate of service as the **company clerk read the roll. Rather worn-looking after their long and circuitous cruise from France, the Marines finally stowed their gear and headed for home.** ***Painting by Colonel Charles H. Waterhouse, USMC Retired. US Marine Corps Art Collection***

required for Marine service. A bitter debate dragged on for several years, during which US Navy Master Commandant David Conner supported Jackson by successfully completing a cruise in the sloop-of-war *Erie* without a Marine guard, while the Military Affairs Committee in the House of Representatives ruled it was out of order to interfere with the status of the Corps. Finally Congress passed 'An Act for the Better Organization of the Marine Corps' on 30 June 1834. As a result, the Marines were not only saved but increased to an unprecedented peacetime strength of sixty-three officers and 1,224 enlisted men. Furthermore, Archibald Henderson was promoted to the rank of colonel.

In response to a presidential order issued during the same year, the Marine Corps adopted a new uniform consisting of a grass green coat with buff facings and light grey trousers, which distinguished it from the Army, and echoed the Revolutionary days of the Continental Marines. Unfortunately the clothing bureau at Philadelphia was unable to acquire a green cloth of sufficient durability. The coats issued to the Marines were found to quickly fade in the sun, especially at sea, and by 1840 the Corps was back in navy blue coats with scarlet facings and sky blue or white trousers.

GONE TO FIGHT THE INDIANS

The Indian policy of President Jackson provided the Marines with the next opportunity for active service. The cause of the conflict which flared up in the Southeast was the government's policy of resettling Native Americans west of the Mississippi River in order to open up their land to white settlers. Although some of the tribes capitulated without much resistance, the Seminole in the Florida Everglades refused to move and in December 1835 attacked the American army posts northwest of Tampa Bay. By April 1836, further trouble had developed as war broke out along the Chattahoochee River between the Creek and the settlers of Georgia and Alabama.

With its Army resources stretched to the limit, the War Department appealed for more troops, and Archibald Henderson responded by offering the services of those Marines stationed in the barracks at the Navy Yard in Washington. Legend has it that, prior to departure in June, Henderson tacked a notice to the front door of the Marine Corps Headquarters building which announced: 'Gone to fight the Indians. Will be back when the war is over.'

Dressed in white fatigue uniforms, Henderson's Marine 'regiment' of thirty-eight officers and about four hundred men arrived too late to see any action against the Creeks, and spent the remainder of the summer patrolling the Georgia/Alabama border on both foot and by steamboat. Taken further south to Florida in September 1836 as part of the force commanded by General Thomas Jesup, the Marines took part in a fight with the Seminoles on 27 January 1837 as part of a composite brigade under Henderson, which also consisted of Army regulars, Georgia volunteers, and friendly Creeks. The Americans attacked a Seminole village near the Hatchee-Lustee River and captured some women and children, Black slaves, and supplies. Meanwhile the Marines were ordered to pursue the Seminole warriors as they retreated into the swampland. Chasing them relentlessly across two streams, a number of Seminole were wounded

Above, Archibald Henderson, the fifth Commandant of the USMC, served for thirty-nine years from 1820 to 1859, and did more than any other individual to form the character of the Marine Corps. He fought aboard the *Constitution* in 1815, and eventually became known as 'the Grand Old Man' of the Corps.
Private Collection, Courtesy of Museums Branch, USMC

Above right, Mameluke sword carried by Brigadier General Commandant Archibald Henderson. Carried by all Marine officers from 1826 until 1859, this type of sword was patterned on that presented to Lieutenant Charles O'Bannon in 1805 for the part he played in the attack on Derna.
USMC Air-Ground Museum, courtesy of Ken Smith-Christmas

before the Marines eventually lost contact with them in another swamp.

Having led one of the few successful engagements of the Seminole campaign, Henderson was brevetted a brigadier general, and as such became the first general in the history of the Marine Corps. As a result of the action subsequently known as the Battle of Hatchee-Lustee, the Seminole chiefs finally agreed to move their people to a reservation. With the war presumably over, Henderson started back for Washington on 22 May, leaving a two-company battalion of Marines in Florida under Lieutenant Colonel Samuel Miller. A week later, seven hundred Seminoles awaiting transportation at Tampa were spirited away by Chief Osceola, and the war was on again. Fighting continued for another five years until Osceola was finally killed in the summer of 1842. Meanwhile, Miller's battalion, which mainly served as depot guards and mounted patrols, was relieved from duty in 1838 and returned north.

The importation of slaves to the US had been banned in 1808, but slaves continued to be run illegally into the country during the following years. In order to investigate slaver activity, Marines from the Navy's Africa Squadron were sent ashore in Liberia in 1843 to question the Berribees, a tribe known to be involved in the slave trade. When Commodore Matthew C. Perry, younger brother of Oliver Hazard Perry, was attacked, a Marine sergeant shot dead the Berribee chief, Ben Crack-

O, and a general struggle ensued. The Marines went on to subdue the whole tribe without a single casualty, and continued to see periodic action along the African coast until the beginning of the American Civil War.

HALLS OF MONTEZUMA

An inevitable result of the westward expansion which had been taking place since 1814 was war between Mexico and the US. The first Americans to set foot on Mexican soil after the Battle of Resaca de la Palma on 9 May 1846, were Marine skirmishers in a naval force under Captain J. H. Aulick, which occupied Burrita some fifteen miles north of the mouth of the Rio Grande. Throughout the remainder of the war, the Marine Corps played an important role on both Mexican coasts within forces which landed at places such as Tampico, San Juan Bautista, Yerba Buena, and Los Angeles.

On 3 March 1847, Archibald Henderson received permission to raise a Marine regiment, but reluctance on the part of Commodore Matthew Perry to relinquish control of the Marines within the Gulf Coast naval brigade prevented the realisation of this project, and only a Marine battalion finally arrived to take part in the siege of Veracruz on 1 July 1847. Attached to Scott's army within the division of General John A. Quitman, this unit was initially commanded by Lieutenant Colonel Samuel E. Watson, who was succeeded by Major Levi Twiggs.

Members of the Marine Battalion took part in the assault on Chapultepec Castle, later misnamed 'the Halls of Montezuma', on 13 September 1847. Major Twiggs, armed with his favourite double-barrelled fowling piece, had overall command of the storming parties for the attack from the south, while Captain John C. Reynolds, a company commander and one of the ablest officers in the Corps, led the first wave, made up of forty Marine and Army volunteers. Indicative of the bravery of the Marines at Chapultepec is the fact that thirteen of the

First Lieutenant Daniel J. Sutherland was photographed in 1847 wearing the M1840 dark blue dress uniform, and holding a Mameluke sword across his lap. Sutherland later became the Quartermaster of the Marine Corps and, in 1857, was responsible for the establishment of its first Depot of Supplies in a four-story house at 226 South 4th Street in Philadelphia. *Photograph from the collection of Dr.William Schultz*

Colonel John Harris, Marine Commandant from 1859 to 1864. As a new second lieutenant in 1814, Harris had fought at Bladensburg, and was breveted for bravery alongside Archibald Henderson at Hatchee-Lustee, Florida in 1837. He wears the uniform for Commandant adopted in 1859, which consisted of a dark blue, double-breasted, frock coat trimmed on collar and cuffs with gold lace loops piped with scarlet. *Photograph courtesy of David M. Sullivan*

twenty-three Marine officers present received brevets. Among the officers killed that day was Major Twiggs and the Commandant's son, Second Lieutenant Charles A. Henderson.

Later the same day, the Marine Battalion was among the first American troops to fight their way into Mexico City. After the Mexican surrender, the Marines were given the task of clearing the *Palacio Nacional* of plunderers and vagabonds while, atop the building, Second Lieutenant A. S. Nicholson, who later became the Adjutant and Inspector General of the Corps, cut down the Mexican tricolor and ran up the Stars and Stripes.

The battle for Mexico City inspired an unknown Marine to compose several lines of verse beginning 'From the Halls of Montezuma', and continuing with the words of the Corps flag inscription 'To the Shores of Tripoli'. On return to barracks after the war, Commandant Henderson was presented by the citizens of Washington D.C. with a new set of blue and gold colours emblazoned with the fuller motto: 'From Tripoli to the Halls of Montezuma.' Later in the 1880s, these lines were set to a march tune taken from Offenbach's comic opera *Genevieve de Brabant*, and eventually became known as the 'Marine Hymn', which today is recognized as one of the foremost service songs.

In the years following war with Mexico, a three-fold increase in American foreign trade kept the US Navy and Marine Corps very busy. Along the

This lithograph of Marines and seamen landing in the Tabasco River near San Juan Bautista during the Mexican War in 1847, by Lieutenant Henry Walke, USN, is the earliest known contemporary illustration showing Marines hitting the beach.
US Naval Institute

coast of South America, Marines were landed at Buenos Aires in 1852 to protect American lives and property from rioters. Later the same year they helped fight a fire that threatened to devour San Juan del Sur in Nicaragua. Between 1856 and 1860, the Marines saw repeated service in the southern part of Nicaragua protecting the workers of an American company building a railroad across the Isthmus of Panama.

A battalion of two hundred Marines commanded by Major Jacob Zeilin accompanied Commodore Perry on his historic expedition across the Pacific to open relations with Japan in 1853. Unsure what reception to expect on landing at Yedo (Tokyo today), Perry sent Zeilin's battalion ashore with orders to either fight or parade. Responding to a peaceful welcome, the Marines lined Perry's route to the ceremonial pavilion dressed in their blue jackets, white trousers, cross-belts, and tall shakoes. About ninety years later, at the end of the Pacific War, ships' Marine detachments would emulate Zeilin's achievement by landing at Yokosuka in Tokyo Bay on 30 August 1945.

In 1854, a sergeant's guard of Marines from the American sloop *Plymouth* joined with Royal Marines and seamen from a British man-of-war

to protect the foreign concessions at Shanghai in China during the Taiping Rebellion. Marines from the *Powhatan* took part in a combined American-British operation against a pirate base in Ty-Ho Bay, near Hong Kong, during the following year. Seventeen Chinese junks were captured in the ensuing two-day sea fight, with the loss of two Marines and three US Navy sailors killed.

Marines became involved in the fiercest fighting since the Mexican War in 1856. When guns from the 'Barrier Forts' in the treaty port of Canton fired on boats from the sloop *Portsmouth,* the American East India Squadron sailed up the Pearl River and landed 287 sailors and Marines, who systematically captured all four forts, spiking numerous cannon, and killing about 500 Chinese defenders, at a loss of seven Americans killed and 20 wounded. When about 2,000 Chinese counter-attacked from a nearby village they were twice repulsed by the Marine detachment under Captain J. D. Simms, who had earlier won his brevet for bravery at Chapultepec.

The Marines next saw significant service on the doorstep of their own headquarters. On 1 June 1857, political unrest broke out in the District of Columbia when the nativist or 'Know-Nothing' faction of Washington imported a gang of roughs called 'Plug-Uglies' from Baltimore to disrupt elections due to take place that day. Armed with horse-pistols, iron bars, sacks filled with stones, and axes, they quickly put the local police to flight. When they next produced a shotted brass cannon, the Mayor of Washington appealed to President James Buchanan for help and the Marine headquarters battalion was called out from its nearby barracks. Drawing up close by the principal polling place in Northern Liberties Market, the Marines under Major Henry B. Tyler confronted the armed mob. During a momentary lull, an old gentleman dressed in civilian clothing and a top hat strode out into the square between the two groups. Waving a gold-headed cane, he rounded on the 'Plug Uglies' behind the cannon, shouting: 'Men, you had better think twice before you fire this piece at the Marines.' Closer examination revealed the speaker to be none other than 74-year old Marine Commandant Archibald Henderson, and the cane he carried was made from the timber of HMS *Cyane,* captured by his ship *Constitution* in 1812!

As the mob milled around indecisively, a squad of Marines rushed the cannon and dragged it clear. What happened next is uncertain. According to a report in the Washington *Star,* a rough attempted to approach with an aimed pistol, and the 'general seized the villain and marched him off to the mayor,

Marines under a cavalry officer, Lieutenant Colonel Robert E. Lee, storm the engine house at Harpers Ferry, Virginia, on 18 October 1859. The ladder used to batter down the doors is seen lying in the foreground. Abolitionist leader John Brown received a sword thrust to his neck from Marine Lieutenant Israel Greene during the ensuing struggle. Taken prisoner, Brown was subsequently tried and hanged. *The Granger Collection, New York*

into whose hands he placed him'. Other sources indicate that Henderson realised violence was unavoidable and walked briskly back to join the ranks of his Marines as the pistol fire increased. The Marines continued to hold their fire until a private was badly wounded in the cheek, at which point they poured in an answering volley. Seeing the Marines reloading their Model 1842 muskets, the mob took to their heels and fled, and order was restored to the capital.

On 6 January 1859, Archibald Henderson died. Known latterly as the 'Grand old Man', he had held his post for 39 years and became one of the greatest Commandants of the Marine Corps. Next in seniority, 66 year-old Lieutenant Colonel John Harris was duly appointed as Colonel-Commandant. Commissioned during the War of 1812, a company commander in the Seminole War, and battalion commander during the Mexican War, he had won two brevets for bravery, but ultimately Harris failed to earn the respect of his predecessor.

Two months before he died, Henderson convened a board of officers to revise the uniform of the Marine Corps, and one of the first acts of his successor was to transmit its findings to the Navy Department. Approved on 24 January 1859, these new uniform regulations were put into practice immediately and remained in effect with only small modifications until 1875. As a result, the Marines did away with their antiquated full dress consisting of leather bell-crowned shako and dark blue swallow-tailed coat, and adopted in its place a nattier Model 1856 black cloth 'uniform cap' and dark blue double-breasted frock coat with collar

A plate from the *Uniform and Dress of the United States Marine Corps*, adopted on 24 January 1859, showing the uniforms (left to right) of Sergeant Major, Chief Musician, Drum Major, and Musician. These regulations remained in effect with only slight modification until 1875. *US Marine Corps Art Collection*

and cuffs edged in red. A less elaborate frock coat, double-breasted for officers and single-breasted for men, was prescribed for undress, with trimmings limited to a red welt in the seam at the base of the collar. A dark blue cloth 'fatigue cap' of French chasseur pattern with straight visor was also worn for undress. Marines aboard sea-going vessels were additionally provided with a dark blue flannel 'fatigue sack' fastened by four small buttons. White cross belts remained the distinctive feature of the Marines throughout this period.

CIVIL WAR

On Sunday night, 16 October 1859, the abolitionist John Brown and his small 'army' of 22 men captured the United States Arsenal at Harpers Ferry, Virginia, in a vain attempt to incite an armed slave rebellion. Quickly surrounded by local militia, Brown and his followers took hostages which included Colonel Lewis Washington, great-grandnephew of George Washington, and fortified themselves in a near by brick-built fire engine house. Shortly after noon the next day, Colonel Harris received an order from Secretary of the Navy Isaac Toucey to send 'all the available Marines at Head Quarters... by this evening's train of cars to Harpers Ferry to protect the public property at that place, which is endangered by a riotous outbreak'.

Within several hours, Lieutenant Israel Greene had 86 Marines plus two 12-pounder Dahlgren howitzers westbound on the Baltimore and Ohio Railroad and headed for the scene of insurrection. One hundred and fifty soldiers from Fort Monroe also received orders to follow, and all were to be commanded by Lieutenant Colonel Robert E. Lee of the 2nd US Cavalry, who was on leave from frontier duty in Texas. The Marines disembarked about a mile short of Harpers Ferry at 10 o'clock that night, where they were joined by Colonel Lee and the bearded Lieutenant J. E. B. Stuart of the 1st US Cavalry, who served as his aide. The Marines were marched across the railroad bridge, and by midnight had occupied the Arsenal grounds where they surrounded the engine house.

Waiting until dawn the next day, Lee held a council of war with his fellow officers. With hostages being held by Brown, it was impossible to use the howitzers. Hence he decided to send Lieutenant Stuart under a flag of truce at sunrise to attempt to persuade John Brown to surrender. If this failed, Stuart was to raise his arm as a 'signal', and the Marines would rush the doors of the engine house. Predictably, Brown would not accept Lee's terms, and the assault was begun by twenty-four Marines led by Lieutenant Greene. An eyewitness and correspondent of the Richmond *Daily Dispatch*

recorded: 'Immediately the signal for attack was given, and the marines... advanced in two lines on each side of the door. Two powerful fellows sprang between the lines, and with heavy sledge hammers attempted to batter down the door. The door swung and swayed, but appeared to be secured with a rope, the spring of which deadened the effect of the blows. Failing thus to obtain a breach, the marines were ordered to fall back, and twenty of them took hold of a ladder, some forty feet long, and advancing at a run, brought it with tremendous power against the door. At the second blow it gave way, one leaf falling inward in a slanting position. The marines immediately advanced to the breach, Major Russell [the Corps Paymaster who, as a staff officer, could not command] and Lieutenant Greene leading the way. A marine in the front fell; the firing from the interior is rapid and sharp, they fire with deliberate aim, and for the moment the resistance is serious and desperate enough to excite the spectators to something like a pitch of frenzy. The next moment the marines pour in, the firing ceases, and the work was done, whilst the cheers rang from every side, the general feeling being that the marines had done their part admirably.'

During the *melée,* John Brown was wounded by a thrust from Israel Greene's dress sword, while all but two of his men were either killed or captured. Hauled out and laid on a mattress, Brown later declared: 'You may dispose of me very easily. I am very nearly disposed of now; but this question is still to be settled—this Negro question, I mean. The end is not yet.' It was the end for Irishman Luke Quinn, the only Marine Private killed during the assault. Another 600,000 Americans in either blue or grey uniforms would die during the Civil War fought between 1861-65 before the question of slavery and state rights was finally settled, and the Marines were involved throughout.

Like the other services, the US Marine Corps was crippled by resignations as men went south to join Confederate forces at the beginning of the Civil War. Although few enlisted men quit, 20 officers out of a total of 63 either resigned or were dismissed. They included some of the Corps' most able men, and all but one of these served in the Confederate States Marine Corps at some time during the war. Adjutant and Inspector Henry B. Tyler, a Virginian and veteran of the Creek Indian War and the Washington riot, was commissioned lieutenant colonel and commanded the Confederate Marine battalion at Pensacola. Major George H. Terrett, another Virginian and hero of the Mexican War, became the Confederate line major and was placed in command of the Marine Camp at Drewry's Bluff, near Richmond, Virginia. John D. Simms, Jr., who also served in Mexico and against the Barrier Forts, was assigned to duty at the Gosport Navy Yard in Virginia as 'Commandant of the Post of Marines', and subsequently became second-in-command to Terrett at Drewry's Bluff. Israel Greene served at Confederate Marine headquarters in Richmond throughout the war.

To make up for these losses and meet the demands of wartime, President Abraham Lincoln authorised the US Marine Corps to be increased to 93 officers and 3,074 enlisted men in July 1861. This almost doubled its pre-war strength. Nonetheless, without the offer of a bounty, and with a longer term of enlistment than that for the Volunteer Army, Marine recruits were difficult to obtain. By June 1862, the Corps had only 2,355 men in its ranks. As the Union Navy expanded, Commandant Harris continued to ask Congress for more men, and in 1863 he was granted a paper strength of 3,600 men, while the Corps' actual strength remained at about 3,000. By the war's end it had reached a peak strength of 4,167 officers and men.

The Marines were among the few Regular troops available to the Federal government in 1861. Early in January of that year, Marine detachments from the Washington Navy Barracks were sent to reinforce the Army posts at Fort Washington on the Potomac River and Fort McHenry in Baltimore, a scene of earlier service in 1814. In Florida, Captain Josiah Watson, commanding the Marine detachment at the Pensacola Navy Yard, surrendered on orders, but Marine ships' guards helped reinforce nearby Fort Pickens which was still in Federal hands, three months later. One hundred and fifty Marines were detailed to the Navy Yard at Norfolk, Virginia, on 20 April where they took part in the attempted destruction of eight vessels, plus stores, buildings, equipment, and ordnance.

The Marine Corps' first significant defense of the Union took place during the battle of Bull Run, or First Manassas, on 21 July 1861. When

Major General Irwin McDowell's hastily prepared 35,000-man Federal Army marched south to attack Confederate forces massed around Manassas in northern Virginia on 16 July, Secretary of the Navy Gideon Welles volunteered the Marine battalion at the Washington Navy Barracks for service during the campaign. A product of the 'call to arms' and the expanded Corps, only the commanding officer, Major John G. Reynolds, plus Captain Jacob Zeilin, and three other officers, had any previous war experience. Of the noncommissioned officers, only nine had seen any previous action — and two of these were musicians. The remaining 336 enlisted men were raw recruits of three weeks' service, some of whom had just been issued weapons.

Attached to Colonel Andrew Porter's 1st Brigade of the 2nd Division, the Marines were assigned to follow Captain Charles Griffin's Battery D, 5th US Artillery, an all-mounted regular Army unit. After jogging and stumbling along 'in double quick time' behind Griffin's guns for several hours prior to the commencement of battle on 21 July, the Marines were exhausted even before McDowell's army made contact with the enemy. Porter's brigade was part of the Federal right wing deployed to cross Bull Run at Sudley Springs in order to deliver a flank attack on Confederate positions northwest of Manassas. As such, it was not heavily involved in

Brigadier General Jacob Zeilin, Marine Commandant from 1864 to 1876. A veteran of the Mexican War and China service, Zeilin was wounded at Bull Run in 1861 but recovered to take part in the Siege of Charleston two years later. During his time as Commandant, he introduced annual inspections of all Marine posts, further standardised Upton's Tactics for use with the Corps, and introduced a new uniform. *Photograph courtesy of David M. Sullivan*

the early fighting. However, Reynolds' Marines had difficulty keeping sight of Griffin's battery as it advanced into action, but eventually found the guns on Matthews Hill north of the Warrenton turnpike, from which point they were shelling the Confederate lines to the south.

Formed up in the rear of the battery, the Marines were exposed to 'a galling fire' from the Confederate counter-battery fire but held their ground. In his after battle report, Colonel Porter was to state that although the Marines were recruits, 'through the constant exertions of their officers [they] had been brought to a fine military appearance'. When the enemy fell back across the turnpike to a new position beyond Henry House Hill, McDowell erroneously believed he had won the day and ordered forward Griffin's battery, and that of Captain James B. Ricketts, Battery I, 1st US Artillery, to the top of that hill. The Marine battalion, plus the 11th New York ('The Fire Zouaves'), were also ordered forward as infantry support. Advancing after the guns, the Marines began to sustain their first casualties. Again reforming behind the combined batteries, they next found themselves exchanging volleys at close range with the blue-clad 33rd Virginia, a Confederate regiment mistaken by Federal officers as further friendly infantry support! Subjected to prolonged musketry and artillery fire, the ranks of the Marines were thrice broken that hot July afternoon, only to be rallied and re-formed by the veteran officers and NCOs in the unit. When a sustained Confederate infantry attack finally silenced the two batteries, a general Federal rout ensued and the Marines bravely formed the first rearguard, and held that position near the Stone House until relieved by the 71st New York State Militia.

The Marine battalion left 8 killed, 8 wounded, and 18 missing on the plains of Manassas. Among the seriously wounded was Captain Zeilin, while Second Lieutenant Robert E. Hitchcock had been killed. During the chaos following the Federal rout, much of the Marine unit retained its formation, although some of the raw recruits panicked and joined in with the general stampede back to Washington. The next day, Reynolds reclaimed about 70 of these men from the hands of the provost guard at the Long Bridge leading over the Potomac River before the remains of his battered but valiant little battalion could be marched back into barracks.

AMPHIBIOUS ATTACK

A month later, on 28 August 1861, the seeds of the modern Marine Corps were planted when Flag Officer Samuel F. DuPont sent a combined battalion of soldiers and Marines from the South Atlantic Blockading Squadron ashore in surfboats to capture Fort Clark on the eastern side of Hatteras Inlet. Impressed by the success of this special landing force, DuPont shortly afterwards ordered them ashore to capture Fort Hatteras, thereby completing a first Federal foothold on the North Carolina coast. In need of reinforcements to complete his planned attack on Port Royal, South Carolina, DuPont sent for Reynolds' Marine battalion at Washington.

DuPont's armada consisting of 50 vessels containing 13,000 soldiers, plus the Marine battalion, left Hampton Roads in late October 1861. What this combined naval and Marine amphibious force may have achieved can only be conjectured as, on 1 November, it plunged headlong into a severe gale. Among the vessels damaged was the SS *Governor,* the transport carrying the Marines, which began to sink. Thanks to the desperate efforts of the Marines, who manned the bilge pumps, the *Governor* continued to wallow in the troughs for another two days until the sloop *Sabine* was able to take the survivors off. Although seven Marines drowned attempting to swim across to the rescue vessel, the battalion showed great courage, and the *Governor* remained afloat long enough for Reynolds to recover most of his command's weapons and half their equipment. Nonetheless, the disaster prevented the Marines from taking part in the capture of Port Royal on 7 November 1861, and military minds had to await further proof of their worth as an amphibious assault force.

On 8 March 1862, a new era in sea warfare dawned when the Confederate ironclad CSS *Virginia* steamed out of the captured Norfolk Navy Yard, and headed straight for the Federal wooden ships on blockade duty in Hampton Roads, off the Virginia coast. Shells sent crashing into the *Cumberland* killed 14 of her 46 Marines, commanded by Captain Charles Heywood, the first of these casualties occurring as they were lining up in formation on the foredeck. After ramming and sinking the *Cumberland,* the *Virginia* bombarded and captured the *Congress,* and forced the remaining three blockading frigates aground. Withdrawing with her captain, Franklin Buchanan, wounded, the *Virginia* returned at dawn the next day to find the little Federal ironclad gunboat *Monitor* waiting for her. Although the slugging match which followed resulted in stalemate, the age of ironclad battleships had begun, and the Marines had been involved.

With the Confederate withdrawal from the Norfolk Navy Yard on 9 May 1862, a battalion of

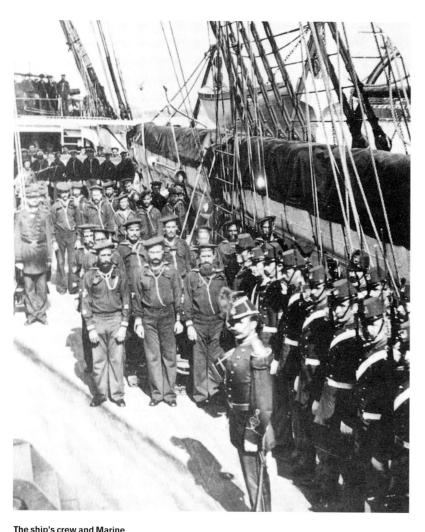

The ship's crew and Marine Guard of USS *Lancaster* on parade in 1883. The officer in the foreground is Captain Henry Clay Cochrane, who had distinguished himself in Alexandria, Egypt, during the previous year. The Marines wear the full dress uniform adopted in 1875. *US Naval Historical Center: NH 381*

200 US Marines under Captain Charles G. McCawley was sent to re-garrison the post. Six days later, the *Monitor,* her sister ironclad *Galena,* and the floating battery *Naugatuck,* probed up the James River and encountered Captain John Simms' battalion of Confederate Marines entrenched at Drewry's Bluff. The *Monitor* was hit repeatedly, while the *Naugatuck's* Parrott gun burst! Aboard the *Galena,* which was also riddled, Marine Corporal John F. Mackie remained on deck firing at the enemy and rallying the vessel's crew. His bravery on 14 March 1862 earned him the Medal of Honor—the first such award received by a United States Marine.

Further south, Flag Officer David G. Farragut, commanding the Western Gulf Blockading Squadron, had forced the mouth of the Mississippi River. Seven Marines died and 19 were wounded as his fleet fought its way passed Forts St. Philip and Jackson, and threatened New Orleans. Men from the remainder of his 333-strong Marine battalion at Farragut's disposal played a vital role in the final capture of the Crescent City. Twenty Marines formed the guard for two navy lieutenants who were sent ashore to demand the city's surrender on 29 April 1862. When the city authorities rejected Federal demands, the fixed bayonets of these Marines shielded the naval officers from the angry mob. Following this, Captain John L. Broome led 250 Marines ashore to seize the Custom House and City Hall. Running up the Union flag over both buildings, they held their ground until the Army arrived several days later.

The battalion of Marines under Major Addison Garland were not quite so fortunate. Embarking on the mail steamer *Ariel* on 1 December 1862, they were assigned as a permanent garrison for the new naval base at Mare Island, California. Six days into her voyage, the *Ariel* was intercepted by the Confederate commerce raider *Alabama* off Cape Maysi, on the eastern tip of Cuba. Garland's Marines ignominiously surrendered their weapons and signed a parole, agreeing not to take up arms against the Confederacy again until properly paroled.

During 1863, Major Zeilin recruited another Marine battalion to assist the South Atlantic Blockading Squadron in its operations against Charleston, South Carolina. Marines from this unit, under Captain Charles G. McCawley, joined a mixed force of sailors and ships' guards which launched a disastrous assault on Fort Sumter on 8 September of that year. Most of the expedition's boats failed to reach the Fort, while the 150 Marines and sailors who succeeded found the Confederates alert and well prepared behind unscalable defences. During the desperate fighting that followed, the battalion quartermaster was killed, three Marines were wounded, and 41 officers and men were captured. Following this fiasco, Zeilin's Marine battalion went into camp on Folly Island and was broken up in early 1864, its members being sent to garrison Navy Yards or to form ships' guards.

Seventy-three year old Colonel John Harris died of fatigue and old age on 12 May 1864, and the Corps was in need of a new Commandant. After a month of deliberation, Secretary of the Navy Welles decided to retire all Marine officers past the legal age, and to recommend the appointment to the post of Jacob Zeilin, who was by then serving as commanding officer of the Barracks at Portsmouth, New Hampshire. On 10 June 1864, Zeilin became the seventh Commandant of the US Marine Corps.

By the end of 1864, the only Confederate port on the Atlantic coast still open to blockade runners was Wilmington, North Carolina, which was defended by the formidable Fort Fisher on Cape Fear. An abortive attack launched by volunteer general Ben Butler on Christmas Eve, was followed by the greatest amphibious battle of the Civil War. A Federal force led by Major General Alfred H. Terry, and composed of the XXIV Army Corps, plus a naval brigade under Commander K. R. Breese consisting of 1,600 sailors and 365 Marines armed with rifled muskets, landed to attack Fort Fisher on 13 January 1865. Deployed as sharpshooters during the advance of Breese's force the next day, the Marines under Captain Lucian L. Dawson were caught up in a generally disorganised assault and found themselves hopelessly dug in at the base of the fort. A few Marines who managed to climb the eight-foot stockade, planted the Stars and Stripes, but were forced to fall back. After several minutes of withering Confederate musketry, the exposed sailors, carrying only 'cutlasses, well sharpened, and... revolvers', broke and ran, taking the Marines with them. Nonetheless, this 'diversionary' attack enabled the Army, assisted by a further force of 180 Marines, to eventually take Fort Fisher, and the grip was finally tightened around the collapsing Confederacy. The Marine battalion under Dawson lost 59 men killed and wounded during the Corps' final major action of the Civil War.

The reputation of the Marines was at a very low ebb after the Civil War. The Corps had not been enlarged significantly, and had not been called upon to perform a prominent amphibious role in the fighting. This was underscored by the fact that, compared with the other services, only 148 Marines had died in battle, while a mere 131 were wounded and 312 died of disease or other causes. This resulted in the introduction of a resolution to Congress on 18 June 1866 to consider 'the expediency of abolishing the Marine Corps, and transferring it to the Army'. After considerable pro-Marine testimony, during which Rear Admiral David Porter stated: 'A ship without Marines is like a garment without buttons', the idea was tabled. Instead the House Naval Affairs Committee recommended the Corps be 'preserved and strengthened' and that Jacob Zeilin, its commanding officer, be promoted to the rank of brigadier general.

On 19 November 1868, a new Marine Corps emblem was adopted which replaced the 'hunter's horn' of the Civil War period. Designed by a board convened on the orders of Jacob Zeilin, it borrowed from the 'globe and laurel' device of the Royal Marines, and consisted of a globe showing the western hemisphere, on top of which was perched an American bald eagle, and behind which was a foul anchor. After some modification, this insignia became common on all Marine uniforms after 1875 and is still worn today.

One of Zeilin's last acts as Commandant, also in 1875, was to approve the adoption of a new uniform for the Marine Corps. Predominantly French in style, officers acquired plumed dress caps and an abundance of gold and mohair braid on the sleeves, chests, and shoulders of their full dress coats. Enlisted men received a shorter blue woolen coat and chasseur-style kepi with lower crown. Leather stocks, which had been on the uniform list for a hundred years, now disappeared forever.

ALWAYS FAITHFUL

In 1876, the Marine Corps motto, which had been 'Fortitudine' since the early 1800s, was changed to 'By Sea and By Land'. Nine years later, Commandant Charles G. McCauley again changed it to 'Semper Fidelis', or 'Always Faithful'. Not entirely unique, as it was shared with the British Devonshire Regiment, the new motto was placed on a ribbon held in the beak of the eagle on the US Marine Corps emblem, and there it remains to this day.

The US Marine Corps band, established in 1798, was in a poor state by 1880. Leader Louis Schneider was dismissed as 'unfit for service', and the future existence of the band was in doubt when John Philip Sousa was appointed in his place, and its future was secured. A prolific composer and accomplished musician, Sousa began to compose marches, recruit new musicians, and change instrumentation, with a confidence which eventually gained international recognition. His composition 'Semper Fidelis' is the only march tune officially authorised by Congress for the US military, and is always used by the Marines for march-past in reviews and parades.

During the latter part of the 19th century, although the Marines played a considerable role in US overseas expansion, the state of the amphibious art stayed at the level of ship's landing parties and provisional battalions. Between 1867 and 1896, the Corps conducted minor landings in locations as far flung as Korea and Egypt. On 30 May 1871, five ships of the Asiatic Squadron conveying the US minister to Seoul, in Korea, were fired on by guns in the forts guarding the approaches to the Han River. A landing force was sent ashore on 10 June, including a two-company battalion of Marines commanded by Captain McLane Tilton. In what became known as the 'Weekend War', three Korean forts were captured, along with 481 antiquated cannon and an array of about 50 very large Korean battle standards. The landing party sustained only 11 casualties, two of them Marines, whilst 243 Koreans were killed. A total of six Marines received Medals of Honor for bravery during the action.

In 1882, the British and French protectorate of the Khedive of Egypt was threatened by a nationalist revolt led by Arabi Pasha. By June of that year, the Royal Navy Mediterranean Fleet had arrived off Alexandria, and close in its wake came the three ships of the US European Squadron, commanded by Rear-Admiral J. W. A. Nicholson. Although much of the trouble had been quelled by 4,000 British troops, including 450 Royal Marines, who had already been landed, a guard of 73 US Marines and 60 sailors under Captain Henry Clay Cochrane, fleet Marine officer, was also sent ashore. The conduct of Cochrane's Marines won the particular admiration of the British as they fought fires, and assisted refugees to sanctuary aboard the American ships. When the forces of Arabi Pasha again approached Alexandria several days later, French and Italian Marines, also present, quickly re-embarked, but Cochrane announced that his party would 'stick by the British and take their chances'. Nothing came of the expected attack, but Cochrane's pluck did not go unnoticed by the British.

In 1884, the US Marines were issued a new rifle, an improved model of the Army's Springfield .45-70 breech-loader, and during the following year had the opportunity to use it in Panama. After the failure of French efforts to build a canal, and with the withdrawal of Colombian troops to quell revolution elsewhere, the region fell under the control of rebels, who began to burn and loot. When Marines under future Commandant, Lieutenant Colonel Charles Heywood landed to protect the US consulate at Aspinwall (now Colón), the Atlantic port on the Isthmus of Panama, correspondent

Richard Harding Davis summed up an era of US gunboat diplomacy when he cabled the London *Times,* 'The Marines have landed and have the situation well in hand'.

On the night of 15 February 1898, an explosion ripped the US battleship *Maine* apart, killing 238 sailors and 28 Marines, as she lay at anchor in Havana harbour. President William McKinley was not keen on war with Spain, but assistant secretary of the Navy Theodore Roosevelt was. Ten days after the sinking of the *Maine,* Roosevelt ordered Commodore George Dewey, Commander-in-Chief of the U.S. Naval Force, Asiatic Station, to proceed with his squadron to the British colony of Hong Kong and there to prepare for action in the Philippines. Two months later, on 24 April, 1898, he finally received instructions to 'commence operations against the Spanish squadron'. Dewey arrived off Manila Bay on 1 May, and after an eight-hour action the ill-prepared Spanish Asiatic Squadron under Admiral Patricio Montojo surrendered. Marines were promptly put ashore to seize the naval base at Cavite, and Dewey was next instructed to await the arrival of the US Army. Later Dewey remarked: 'If there were 5,000 Marines under my command at Manila Bay, the city would have surrendered to me on May 1.'

Opposite, Marines under Captain McLane Tilton land from ships of the Asiatic Fleet to storm the Korean forts on the Salee River during the 'Weekend War' in June 1871.
Painting by Sergeant John Clymer.
USMC Photo #306075

Above, entitled 'The Fight at Guantanamo: Marines under Lieutenant Colonel Huntingdon repelling an attack', this painting by staff artist Frederick Coffey Yohn was originally published in *Colliers Weekly* on 25 June 1898. It depicts the Spanish attack, 11 June 1898, on 636 men of the 1st Marine Division, commanded by

Colonel R. W. Huntington, who had been landed at Guantanamo Bay, Cuba, the day before. Taken by surprise, Marines who had been swimming in the sea can be seen rushing to join their comrades formed into a semicircle on the far slope of the hill to repel the attack.
Jean S. and Frederic A. Sharf collection

The US Marine Corps was increased to the unprecedented size of 119 officers and 4,713 enlisted men following the outbreak of war with Spain. On 10 June 1898, a Marine battalion commanded by Colonel R. W. Huntington landed at Guantanamo Bay, Cuba, in order to secure a coaling station and supply base for the US Fleet then blockading Santiago Harbour. The expedition consisted of 21 Marine officers and 615 enlisted men, plus two Navy officers and two seamen. After establishing a beachhead and holding out against persistent Spanish sniper fire and several night time attacks, Huntington decided to crush Spanish resistance in the area.

Both the Americans and their enemies were hampered by a shortage of water, but the Spanish, who lacked shipboard distilling equipment, were almost entirely dependent upon a well at the village of Cuzco. Hence, on 14 June, two companies of Marines under Captain George F. Elliott, accompanied by about 60 Cuban revolutionary reinforcements, and supported by the guns of the US gunboat *Dolphin,* were ordered to attack a garrison of Spanish regulars, plus some Cuban loyalists, defending the well at Cuzco. Sent ahead to cut off any enemy retreat, Lieutenant Louis J. Magill crested the hill above Cuzco as the *Dolphin* began to shell the Spanish blockhouse and trenches below. Finding themselves directly in the line of fire, most of the Marines hit the deck. Without hesitation, Sergeant John H. Quick jumped up in plain view and began waving an improvised flag in a cease-fire signal to the ship. Calmly remaining exposed, with Spanish Mauser bullets whistling around him, Quick continued to signal until the naval barrage stopped. Quick was one of 15 Marines to win the Medal of Honor for bravery during the short 14-week war with Spain.

In the face of in-coming shells and Marine rifle fire, the Spanish retreated from Cuzco having sustained 40 killed, and one officer and 18 men captured. Such was the first fight between

Top, the Marine Guard of USS *Omaha* parade in undress on deck while their ship is docked at the Portsmouth Navy Yard in New Hampshire, circa 1888. Their sky blue overcoats are worn without detachable cape. Note the inverted chevrons on the lower sleeves of the non-commissioned officers nearest the musicians.
US Naval Historical Center: NH 58909

Middle, this off-duty group of Marines during the Spanish-American War wear a wonderful mixture of clothing. The man second from right, identified as 'Dawson, Co. E, 2nd Regt', has donned his M1892 special full dress uniform, with white linen summer trousers. The others wear M1898 summer field dress, with drab Mills belts and what appear to be cavalry-issue leggings. Note the stack of Lee rifles at left.
USAMHI/photo by Jim Enos

Bottom, on 1 April 1899, Marines from the protected cruiser *Philadelphia* went ashore at Samoa in a combined landing party with Royal Marines to intercede in an argument between two chiefs as to the succession to the Samoan throne. These US Marines man a Colt automatic rifle at the US Consulate established in the rear defense lines at Apia on Upolu Island, Samoa, at this time.
US Military History Institute, Carlisle, Pennsylvania

Americans and Spanish on Cuban soil, and the Marines were there. The story of the action at Cuzco Well was pounced on by the American press, and the 'Marine' became a national hero overnight. On a more serious level, the landing at Guantanamo demonstrated the need for Marines as an assault force to be employed with the fleet, and gave added strength to those who would later advise that the capture and defense of advanced posts should be the primary role of the Marine Corps.

Regarding uniforms, the blue wool field dress was abandoned by the Marine Corps sometime between 10-14 June 1898, and brown linen summer clothing, including a five-button blouse with rolling collar and two flapped breast pockets, was adopted for use by both officers and men. This was worn with a felt olive drab campaign hat, and blue wool, or white linen, shirt. Obviously prompted by their service in the Caribbean and the Pacific, the Corps completed their warm weather uniform change via the 'Regulations of the Uniform Dress of the Marine Corps, 1900', which included a khaki field dress consisting of a single-breasted blouse, with standing collar, pointed cuffs, shoulder straps, and two flapped breast pockets with box plaits. Also introduced at this time was the blue dress uniform which is virtually indistinguishable from that worn by the US Marine Corps today.

During the early months of 1899, rebellion broke out in the Philippines. Having helped the Americans capture Manila, Filipino nationalist leader Emilio Aguinaldo fully expected the government of the Islands to be turned over to him. Instead he was ordered to march his forces out of the city. As fighting intensified, Admiral Dewey cabled a request for Marines, by now armed with the M1898 .30 calibre Krag-Jorgensen rifle, to be sent to protect the naval base at Cavite, in Manila Bay. By the end of 1900, sufficient numbers had been transferred to the Philippines to form the 1st Marine Brigade, consisting of four Marine battalions and two artillery companies.

By the fall of 1901, Aguinaldo had been captured but thousands of Filipinos vowed to continue the struggle to the death. The most fanatical freedom fighters were the *Moro,* or Mohammedan Filipinos. The US Army was having difficulty controlling these religious fanatics, who had massacred 38 members of the 9th US Infantry at Balangiga on Samar Island. Marines under Major Littleton W. T. Waller were sent from Cavite to deal with the situation and, in a combined operation with the Army, managed to pin down and capture about 3,000 *Moro* in a jungle stronghold in the cliffs above the Sojoton River. Waller was next ordered to reconnoitre a telegraph route from Lanang to Basey, a distance of about 52 miles, but the ill-fated expedition was beset by disaster, as boats sank in treacherous rivers, provisions were lost, and bearers mutinied. Ten Marines died during the long march, which eventually achieved its objective. Later it became a custom in the messes of the Marine brigade to honour and toast the surviving officers of the Samar battalion with the tribute: 'Stand gentlemen, he served on Samar'.

RIGHTEOUS FISTS

During the summer of 1900, and prior to the extensive build up of Marines in the Philippines, the 'Boxer Rebellion' had broken out, as the 'Righteous Fists of Harmony', or 'Boxers', began their efforts to expunge the 'foreign devils' from North China. On 29 May, Marines and sailors from the battleship *Oregon* and the cruiser *Newark* landed at Taku and sailed up the Heilho River on commandeered junks. Arriving at Tientsin, 49 Marines under Captains John T. ('Handsome Jack') Myers and Newt H. Hall entrained for Peking with forces from other nations. Shortly after reaching its destination, the Boxers tore up the railroad tracks, and this small international force found itself cut off and surrounded.

By 10 June, an eight-nation 2,500-man relief column was formed in Tientsin under Vice-Admiral

Next page, **Marine Corps recruiting posters used in 1918: (left) artist James Montgomery Flagg shows a Marine in summer field service uniform; (right) Captain John Thomason Jr.'s artwork depicts a 'Leatherneck' in Army field service dress after arrival in the trenches.** *Peter Newark's Military Pictures*

BE A U.S. MARINE!
307 Evening Star Building, Washington, D. C.

LET'S
GO!

U·S·MARINES

Sir Edward Seymour, RN. The American contingent, which included a few Marines, was commanded by US Navy Captain Bowman H. McCalla. Repairing the railroad track as it went, this force also encountered fierce resistance and took refuge in a fortified arsenal only six miles north of Tientsin. Towards the end of the month, another relief column which included a 400-strong Marine battalion from the Philippines under Major Waller, managed to drive back the Boxer hordes and relieved Seymour's beleauguered men.

In Peking, the siege of the Legation Quarter began in earnest on 20 June. About 3,000 people, jammed into an area three-quarters of a mile square, came under constant attack for 55 days until finally rescued by an 18,000-strong relief force. During the ensuing siege, a number of Marines distinguished themselves. On 3 July, Captain Myers led a party of 30 US Marines, 25 Royal Marines, and 16 Russian soldiers to retake part of the defences lost two days before.

Engaging in hand-to-hand fighting, they killed 30 Boxers and captured two flags. Two US Marines were killed and several were wounded during this action — including 'Handsome Jack' Myers. Twelve days later, Private Daniel J. Daly of Glen Cove, New York, distinguished himself by giving covering fire all night long as builders repaired the eastern gate. Also stopping several Boxer sorties along the wall, his bravery won him his first Medal of Honor on this occasion. Given the same award for service in Haiti in 1915, Daly became the only enlisted Marine ever to win the Medal of Honor for two separate actions.

When the relief column finally reached the outskirts of Peking on 13 August, two companies of the 451 US Marines in its ranks scaled the city wall south of the Tung Pien Gate. During this action, Lieutenant Smedley Butler, who left a hospital bed to join the expedition, came close to death when a bullet glanced off a button on his blouse, apparently rearranging South America on the Marine 'globe and anchor' tattoo on his chest! At the end of the

A typical recruit at Norfolk, Virginia, in 1917. At this time recruit companies were identified by letter, line companies by number, on their campaign hats.
John A. Stacey collection

A Marine detachment and sergeant wearing the khaki field dress prescribed in the 1900 Uniform Regulations. This image was probably taken between 1906 and 1908 as the men carry .30-calibre M1903 Springfield rifles, but NCOs' chevrons are not yet converted to the khaki called for in the 1908 Regulations.
John A. Stacey collection

fighting, of about 500 Legation defenders, 55 had been killed and 135 wounded, but the rebellion had been crushed. Of the 56 US Marines and sailors in the Quarter, 17 were casualties.

The Marines fought alongside the 2nd Battalion, Royal Welch Fusiliers at Tientsin and Peking, and a lasting friendship was formed. Since then on St. David's Day, and the Marine Corps birthday, the two units exchange greetings and the watchword '...and St. David'. Furthermore, at the behest of the First Marine Battalion, Bandleader Sousa composed the march 'The Royal Welch Fusiliers' to commemorate the occasion.

During the first two decades of the 20th century, the Marines continued to make their mark around the world—landing in such places as Panama, to protect workers on the canal; in Nicaragua, to demonstrate American support for the Catholic moderates as election rioting broke out; in Ethiopia, to protect a diplomatic mission; and in Cuba, to put down a black revolt.

In 1914, tension between the US and Mexico led to renewed war between the two nations. Since the death of President Porfirio Diaz, Victoriano Huerta had made himself a dictator. On 9 April, the paymaster and boat crew from the USS *Dolphin* went ashore at Tampico to buy gasoline and were promptly thrown in jail. Although they were released immediately, Rear Admiral Henry T. Mayo was not satisfied and demanded a 21-gun salute to the American flag. Upon Huerta's refusal, the US imposed a blockade on Mexico's Gulf ports, and the Marine 'Advance Base Force', organised in 1900 under Colonel John A. Lejeune, took station off Veracruz. On 20 April, President Woodrow Wilson received news that a German freighter was headed for Veracruz laden with arms for Huerta, and immediately issued the order: 'Take Veracruz at once.' At dawn the next day, the 2nd Marine Regiment commanded by Lieutenant Colonel Wendall C. 'Buck' Neville, and armed with Model 1903 Springfield rifles, landed and seized the

cable station and power plant. By midday a fierce fire fight had developed in the railroad yards as Marine reinforcements poured in. House-to-house fighting continued the next day until, by 24 April, Veracruz had been pacified, at a cost of 135 Marine and naval casualties. An Army brigade under Brigadier General Frederick Funsten relieved most of the Marines five days later, and Huerta's regime was replaced by that of the more liberal President Carranza. The success of Lejeune's 'Advanced Base Force' at Veracruz further convinced the American military fraternity that the Marine Corps had a permanent place in the US armed forces.

The combined effect of German unrestricted U-boat warfare and British naval interception of the Zimmerman telegram encouraging Mexico to attack the US, finally persuaded President Wilson to declare war on Germany and the Central Powers on 6 April 1917, and the Marines found themselves involved in the Great War. By that time, the actual strength of the Corps, including the newly created

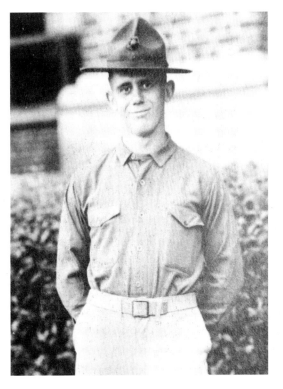

Sergeant Raymond I. Hollan, 5th Company, 1st Marines, at Philadelphia in 1919. Hollan wears summer field service dress. The khaki flannel shirt worn was introduced in 1904, and buttons down the entire front, as opposed to the Army-issue pull-over pattern. His web belt was adopted during the same year, and the same pattern remains in use today.

Detail showing 'globe, eagle, and anchor' device, and company number on the campaign hat worn by Sergeant Hollan.
John A. Stacey collection

Marine Corps Reserve, had risen to 511 commissioned and warrant officers, and 13,214 enlisted men. Determined they would be among the 'First to Fight', Marine Commandant General George Barnett ensured that Colonel Charles Doyen's 5th Marine Regiment was aboard the transport USS *Henderson* when it sailed on 14 June 1917 as part of the first US convoy carrying the American Expeditionary Force (AEF), to France. Once 'Over There', Doyen's Marines expected to remain together and train as a single unit for front line action, but were disappointed to find themselves being parceled out along the length and breadth of France as military police and line-of-communication troops.

With the arrival of the 6th Marines and the 6th Machine Gun Battalion by early 1918, the Marines were finally brought together as the 4th Brigade, 2nd Division, under Doyen, who had been promoted to brigadier general. To simplify the problem of supply, the Marine Brigade in France, consisting of 280 officers and 9,164 men, were ordered to wear olive drab instead of the forest green winter field uniform adopted in 1914. They also exchanged their beloved field hats for Army-style overseas caps, and wore the steel helmet, or 'dishpan', in battle for the first time.

DEVIL DOGS

The Marines first saw action in the sector of trenches northwest of Chateau-Thierry during June 1918, where they filled a gap left by a retreating French unit on the edge of the Bois de Belleau. When advised by a passing French officer that he too should withdraw, Marine Captain Lloyd Williams replied: 'Retreat, hell. We just got here!' The Germans launched a major attack on this position on 3 June and felt the effect of Marine marksmanship before they came within 800 yards of the American lines. Reporting back to headquarters that they had encountered 'shock troops', the Germans dubbed the Marines *teufelhunden,* or 'devil dogs', and the Marines revelled in the name!

At daybreak on 6 June 1918, the 4th Brigade was ordered 'over the top' to drive the Germans out of Belleau Wood and the village of Bouresches. Advancing across open wheatfields without adequate artillery covering fire, the 1st Battalion, 5th Marines, was almost annihilated, only a handful of men reaching a prominence referred to as Hill 142, a half mile to the north. The second phase attack began late that afternoon, when the 3rd Battalion, 5th Marines and the 2nd and 3rd Battalions, 6th Marines, attacked into Belleau Wood itself. Approaching across less exposed

terrain, they fell upon the German machine gun nests and drove the supporting infantry from their positions. During this attack, several veteran Marines further distinguished themselves. John Quick, by now a 45-year old Sergeant Major, gained the Army's Distinguished Service Cross for driving a Model 'T' Ford truck loaded with small-arms ammunition through intense German fire, in order to re-supply elements of the 6th Marines. On another part of the battlefield, Gunnery Sergeant Dan Daly was heard to yell to his platoon as he led a charge: 'Come on, you sons of bitches! Do you want to live forever?' Twice wounded at Belleau Wood, Daly was eventually awarded the Navy Cross, the Distinguished Service Cross, two Purple Hearts, the French Médaille Militaire, the Croix de Guerre, and the French Victory Medal! By dusk on that fateful June day in 1918, 1,087 Marines lay dead or wounded—a figure not to be eclipsed until the 2nd Marine Divison hit the beaches of Tarawa in November 1943.

The battle of Belleau Wood was to drag on until 26 June 1918, when further Marine assaults finally drove the last Germans out of their positions, and Brigadier General James G. Harbord, by then commanding the 4th Brigade, received the signal: 'Belleau Woods now U.S. Marine Corps entirely.'

Following the action between 6-26 June 1918, Belleau Wood was referred to in all official French reports of the battle as 'Bois de la Brigade de Marine'. Furthermore, the battalions that fought through those fateful days were decorated by the French. Every Marine involved was entitled to wear on his shoulder a *fourragére,* or braided cord, indicating bravery in battle. To this day, members of those regiments are still authorised to wear the award.

Another abiding by-product of the battle of Belleau Wood was the introduction of a new term in the soldier's vocabulary. The shallow rifle pits scratched out in the front line were dubbed 'foxholes' by the Marines. A news correspondent heard the term and reported it, and the era of the foxhole was born.

Marine Corps aviation originated in 1912 when Lieutenant Alfred A. Cunningham made his first solo flight at Marblehead, Massachusetts, lasting two hours and 40 minutes. Joining the Chambers Board following this, Cunningham and five naval officers drew up 'a comprehensive plan for the organization of a naval aeronautical service'. As developments unfolded, Marine volunteers took part in experiments such as bombing from a naval plane; taking off by catapult from a battleship underway; and looping a seaplane.

By early 1918, the 1st Marine Aviation Force of

four squadrons had been formed with Cunningham as commander. Arriving at Brest on 30 July 1918, they first flew American-built de Havilland-4 pursuit bombers, or 'Flying Coffins', and then were transferred to RAF squadrons where they flew the more reliable British de Havilland DH-9 and Sopwith Camel. During the remaining weeks of the war, Cunningham's Marine airmen attacked retreating German ground forces, duelled with enemy fighter planes, and flew photo-reconnaissance missions. At the end of hostilities, the 1st Marine Aviation Force was credited with shooting down 12 enemy planes, dropping 52,000 pounds of bombs during 57 raids, and inflicting 330 German casualties.

Meanwhile, back in the trenches the Germans launched their last offensive of the war, striking towards Soissons on 15 July 1918—and the Marines were in their way. The 5th Marines were in the front line with the 6th Marines held in reserve, and both were soon in the thick of battle. With his trench sector under heavy attack, Company commander Captain Clifton Cates advised headquarters: '…I have only two men left out of my company and 20 out of other companies… I will hold.' A total of 1,972 Marines were either dead or wounded during the two day battle of Aisne-Marne.

Despite such distinguished conduct, the Marines

Veterans of the Great War. Officers of Marine Company E, 3rd Army Composite Regiment. This regiment was formed in 1919 for ceremonial purposes, and was composed of companies from each 2nd Division line unit which served in France. The officer third from the right, wearing puttees, is Captain Clifton B. Cates, hero of the Aisne-Marne battle, and later USMC Commandant from 1948 to 1952.
John A. Stacey collection

in France were not favoured by General John Pershing, commander of the AEF, who doubted the wisdom of keeping them together as a separate division. Later, on receipt of disappointing Army battle reports, Pershing was forced to observe: 'Why in hell can't the Army do it if the Marines can? They are all the same kind of men. Why can't they be like Marines?' On 28 July 1918, he placed Marine General John Lejeune in command of the Second Division, marking the first time that a Marine officer would lead Army units.

After receiving replacements to reinforce its depleted ranks, the 4th Marine Brigade took part in the assault on St. Mihiel on 12 September 1918. Opening the American Meuse-Argonne offensive, the last major battle of the war, the Marines overwhelmed the German defenders and St. Mihiel was taken. This offensive went on for 47 days and involved a total of 550,000 American troops, and still remains the largest land battle in US military history. During the attack on Blanc Mont from 2-9 October 1918, the 'devil dogs' led the way, advancing nine kilometres in a single day and capturing 1,700 Germans. Crossing the Meuse River under cover of darkness on 10 November, the Marines resumed their attack at dawn—only to learn that an armistice had been agreed, and the war ended at 11 a.m. the next day.

During the war, a total of 78,839 Marines served in the Corps, while about 32,000 of these saw action in Europe with the AEF, and 1,600 performed naval duty ashore. The Marines who fought in France within the 4th Brigade sustained 11,366 casualties, of which 2,459 were killed or missing in action. Only 67 Marines were taken prisoner. In the words of Colonel A. W. Catlin, commanding officer of the 6th Marines: 'Surrendering wasn't popular!'

The enormous expansion of the Corps caused the creation of a wartime Marine Corps Reserve with 496 officers and 6,760 enlisted personnel. On 12 August 1918, the Secretary of the Navy authorised Commandant Barnett to enroll women as reservists, and the next day, Opha Mae Johnson, became the first woman Marine. Known as 'skirt Marines' or 'Marinettes', a total of 305 female Reservists had entered the Marine Corps as clerks to 'Free a Marine to Fight' by the end of the war. They were all ordered out of service in 1919.

As a result of their participation in the Great War, the Marines were catapulted into the limelight, having shown their combat effectiveness at Belleau Wood, Soissons, and St. Mihiel. The 4th Brigade remained in Europe as part of the Army of Occupation until 12 August 1919, when it returned home. After they had passed him in review in Washington, President Wilson commented: 'The whole nation has reason to be proud of them.'

Nonetheless, post-war Marine strength was reduced to 17,047. Once again the Corps had become a small and exclusive military fraternity. During the next two decades, while the US pondered isolationism, and was crippled by the Wall Street Crash and ensuing economic depression, the Marine Corps continued to protect American interests in Latin America, the Caribbean, and China. As the 1930s wore on and war clouds loomed again in Europe, the Marine Corps began to expand once more, reaching a strength of about 64,000 when, on 7 December 1941, the Japanese attacked Pearl Harbor. During 90 minutes, 300 Japanese carrier-based planes destroyed much of the US Pacific fleet. In the American Pacific campaign which followed, the US Marine Corps at last came into its own as one of the world's elite fighting forces, expanding to a maximum strength of 485,833 by 1945, and developing the fighting qualities and tenacity for which it is renowned today.

Officer, NCOs, and other enlisted men at Marine Barracks, Quantico, in 1922. The *fourragère* worn with their undress uniforms indicate that all were members of the 4th Marine Brigade which served in France during World War One.
John A. Stacey collection

ARMING
THE MARINES

According to historian and former Marine Allan Millett, victory in the Pacific was won by 'the individual rifleman. Barely out of boyhood, often scared and sometimes blindly heroic, he fought and conquered—and created the image of the modern Marine Corps. On his head rests a helmet covered with camouflage cloth; his light green cotton dungarees with the black USMC globe and anchor on the left pocket are stained and often bloody; his M-1 is scratched but clean; his leggings (if he still has them) cover soft brown work shoes; around his waist hangs a cartridge belt carrying two canteens, a first aid packet, and a K-Bar knife. Burned by the tropic sun, numbed by the loss of comrades, sure of his loyalty to the Corps and his platoon, scornful of the Japanese but wary of their suicidal tactics, he squints into the western sun and wonders what awaits him. Ahead lie Peleliu, Iwo Jima, and Okinawa.'

The Marines who fought the Pacific War between 1941 and 1945 looked very different from this at the beginning of the conflict. Based predominantly on the 1937 Regulations, the uniform worn at Pearl Harbor and Wake Island was essentially the same as their predecessors had taken into the trenches during the First World War. Indeed, some equipment issued in 1940 was left over from 1918. This uniform was to undergo a multitude of amendments as the Corps adapted to the extreme demands of tropical warfare during the course of World War Two.

It is sometimes wrongly assumed that Marines often depended on cast-off Army or Navy clothing. Certainly there were supply shortages, but most items of uniform were of unique design, being manufactured at the Corps' own Quartermaster Department established at Philadelphia in 1880. Weapons and equipage were another matter. Marines often had to wait while other services were supplied first. Indeed, only 5 percent of its equipage was manufactured specifically for or by the Marine Corps, while 65 percent came from Army sources,

five percent from the Navy, and 25 percent was derived from commercial sources. The Corps did not receive the M1 Garand rifle until six years after the Army, but this was partially due to the Marine's reluctance to part with his '03 Springfield'!

UNIFORM

On virtually all occasions the Marines stationed in the Pacific on the eve of the Japanese attack on Pearl Harbor wore what was classified as the summer service uniform. For officers, this consisted of a single-breasted, unlined coat of khaki 'suiting' or gabardine, for garrison duty. This garment was fastened by four equally spaced dull-finish bronze, detachable buttons bearing the Marine Corps 'eagle and anchor' device first adopted in 1821. It had a roll collar and notched lapels, bearing a dull bronze 'eagle, globe and anchor' emblem (with 'anchor inboard'), shoulder straps, and four patch pockets with pointed flaps, each secured by a single smaller button of the same pattern. The two chest pockets had vertical box plaits in the centre, while the two lower pockets were of the bellows pattern. The skirt, which regulations stated was to extend '1 to 2 inches below [the] crotch, according to height of wearer', was slightly flared, and could either be one piece with the body of the coat, or a separate piece joined to the body at the waistline. A straight vent ran from the belt line at the back to the bottom of the skirt. Cuffs were plain, being three inches wide on the under seam, and curving to a point six inches wide on the outer facing side of sleeve. Rank insignia was worn on the shoulder straps.

Worn with the officers' coat was the dark brown 'cordovan', or goatskin, 'Sam Browne' Model 1935 officer's belt with brass fittings and a strap over the right shoulder. Warrant officers wore the same pattern belt without the shoulder strap.

The summer service khaki coat prescribed for enlisted men, of similar pattern to that worn by officers but minus lower patch pockets, ceased to

be issued in 1937 and was seldom seen beyond that date.

Preferred summer service garrison headwear for officers was the wide-crowned cap of the pattern originally introduced in 1912. This had a khaki-coloured satin cover, ribbed band, and looped quatrefoil ornamentation of silk tubular braid on the top of the crown. Attached to the front was the bronze version of the 1936-pattern Marine Corps emblem, usually of two-piece construction. The visor and chin strap were of cordovan, the former being lined with green leather. Senior officers' visors were embellished with gilt-embroidered oak leaves and acorns, or 'scrambled eggs'—two rows for generals, and one for those of field grade. The cap worn by enlisted men was of the same pattern but plain and covered with khaki cotton, with a slightly smaller bronze, one-piece device in front.

On tropical duty, both officers and enlisted men also wore a summer garrison cap, also known as the 'overseas' cap. Made of khaki tan cotton, it had a collar size bronze Marine Corps emblem, anchor forwards, attached to the left side. Officers wore small rank insignia on the right side of this cap. First worn by Marines deployed to Europe during 1917-18, it later became the most common non-combat headgear during World War Two, because it folded conveniently into packs and sea bags.

The khaki cotton shirt, worn by both officers and men, was used for field service as well. Of the same pattern as the khaki flannel version worn with the winter service uniform, it had remained virtually unchanged since its introduction in 1927. Made in two styles, with collar either attached or detached, it was fastened at the front with eight, light brown, vegetable ivory buttons. Its two patch breast pockets had pointed flaps, distinguishing it from the straight Army flaps, which were secured by a single button of the same type, as were the three-inch cuffs. For garrison duty, shirts were worn with a square-cut, tan cotton necktie or 'field scarf', which was kept outside the shirt, as opposed to being

Enlisted men in standard utility (left) and summer service (right) uniforms as prescribed by the 1937 regulations. The utility uniform consisted of one-piece dungarees or coveralls of sage green herringbone twill. Note the black-stencilled acronym 'USMC' on the left breast pocket flap, below which is the eagle, globe, and anchor on the pocket itself. The man in summer service dress wears his tie outside his shirt according to Marine regulations, as opposed to US Army regulations which required that the tie should be tucked in. Both men wear fibre sun helmets with the service cap emblem attached, and field shoes or 'boondockers'.
National Archives
Photo # 127-N-402599

tucked Army-style between the second and third buttons. A brass clasp held the field scarf and collar in place.

When coats were not worn, officers' rank was indicated by small insignia attached each side of the shirt collar, one inch from the front edge. Non-commissioned officers rank was indicated by a complicated series of green-on-tan chevrons, which was much simplified from the beginning of World War Two. A division patch was worn at the top of the left sleeve.

Summer service trousers of khaki-coloured drill, or gabardine, were straight-legged without turn-ups. Those worn by officers had both side and hip pockets, while enlisted men had side pockets only. The fly was closed by five, brown plastic, four-hole buttons. Officers had suspender buttons sewn inside the waist band. All ranks had six $2\frac{1}{2}$- long belt loops through which a khaki cotton web belt, fastened by a blackened metal, open frame buckle, was threaded. The buckle also served as an excellent bottle opener! Officers, and enlisted mens' mounted detachments, could also wear riding breeches of the same colour and material as the trousers, with high-legged boots, either full lace up or strap and buckle.

Officers wore dark brown, cordovan leather leggings, or puttees, for field service. Enlisted men were issued pattern-1936 khaki or tan canvas, leggings of three piece construction with seven eyelets and six hooks, and a woven web canvas instep strap. Shorter canvas leggings, with only six eyelet holes for laces, began to replace the longer ones by 1943. To avoid the 'blousing', or billowing out of trousers over legging tops, regulations prescribed that trousers should be 'folded from underneath over the outside of the leg, with as little fullness at the knees as practicable'. It was common practice in combat for Marines to wear their trousers over the leggings, which prevented water holding in the trousers during beach landings or when fording rivers or creeks. Many men discarded

leggings completely when on active service.

Enlisted men always wore ankle-high, dark brown leather field shoes with the summer service uniform. Most were made under contract by the Hermann Shoe Company of Boston, Massachusetts, which had been associated with the Marine Corps since the beginning of the 20th century. This company went on to produce many of the standard-issue 'boondocker' reversed leather, or suede, side out field shoes worn by all Marines in the Pacific War.

Underwear, which the Marine referred to as his 'skivvies', consisted of standard issue white cotton sweat shirt and shorts, often dyed green in the field. Towards the end of the war these were issued in sage green. Socks were white.

Field headgear for both officers and men consisted of the pattern-1912 broad-brimmed field or 'campaign' hat, the fibre tropical helmet, or the Model 1917A1 steel 'dishpan' helmet. Made of

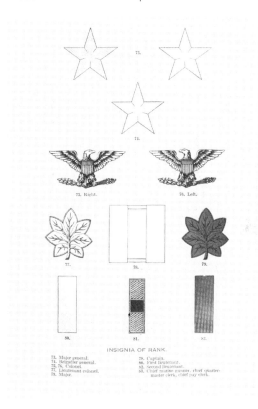

A plate which accompanied the 1937 USMC Uniform Regulations showing officers' rank insignia. Worn on the shoulder straps with summer service uniform, this consisted of two silver stars for major general commandant and other major generals; one star for brigadier general; silver eagle for colonel; silver leaf for lieutenant colonel, and gilt leaf for major; two silver bars for captain; one silver bar for first lieutenant; one gilt bar for second lieutenant; and a gilt bar with medium blue band for chief warrant officer.
Courtesy of John A. Stacey

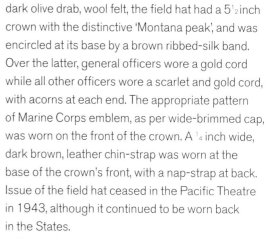

dark olive drab, wool felt, the field hat had a 5½ inch crown with the distinctive 'Montana peak', and was encircled at its base by a brown ribbed-silk band. Over the latter, general officers wore a gold cord while all other officers wore a scarlet and gold cord, with acorns at each end. The appropriate pattern of Marine Corps emblem, as per wide-brimmed cap, was worn on the front of the crown. A ¼ inch wide, dark brown, leather chin-strap was worn at the base of the crown's front, with a nap-strap at back. Issue of the field hat ceased in the Pacific Theatre in 1943, although it continued to be worn back in the States.

The M1917A1 steel helmet, or 'dishpan', was worn by all US troops at the beginning of World War Two. Many were refurbished M1917 helmets supplied by the British government to US forces during World War One. Refurbishment began in January 1936, and involved replacing the old head support with a new suspension lining of soft, padded leather. The old leather chin-strap, which had been attached to the helmet either side by two metal loops, was replaced by a webbing chin-strap fixed directly on to the lining. New 'M1917 helmets' of Hadfield manganese steel were also supplied to order by the McCord Radiator and Manufacturing Company, of Detroit, at the beginning of 1941. Usually painted forest green, they also had a khaki web chinstrap with blackened metal catch and tip. According to the 1937 Marine regulations, this strap was to be 'always worn to the rear', although photographic evidence showing men wearing it under the chin suggests this regulation was generally ignored.

The pre-war sun helmet was designed and intended for field use in place of the steel helmet in tropical climates. Consisting of a rigid fibre shell impregnated with water-repellent materials, it was covered in either tan and olive drab cotton, had a green lined interior, and a cloth chin strap over the front brim. It was worn with a bronze Marine Corps emblem attached to the front. This helmet

Left, the coat worn with the two-piece, herringbone twill, utility uniform issued in 1941. Note the black stencilled acronym 'USMC' and eagle, globe and anchor on the breast pocket. *Photos by the author, courtesy of Jim Moran*

Far left, the standard-issue, rough side out, leather field service shoes with rubber soles and heels. Known as 'boondockers', many pairs of these shoes were made under contract for the Marine Corps by the Hermann Shoe Company of Boston, Massachusetts. *Photos by the author, courtesy of Jim Moran*

disappeared from Pacific service early in the war, but continued to be issued to recruits undergoing training plus other Stateside personnel.

The Marine Corps had used a loose-fitting blue denim fatigue uniform for dirty work details and some field exercises since the 1920s. Known as 'utilities' or 'dungarees', they were either a one-piece coverall or a two-piece bib and brace coverall and coat. The coat with the latter uniform was fastened by four 'USMC' metal buttons, and had three flapless pockets, one being on the left breast, and the other two on the front skirts. During 1940-41, these garments began to be replaced with sage green cotton 'utilities' made of herring bone twill, then a popular material for civilian work clothing, which were available as a one-piece coverall or two-piece uniform.

JUNGLE SUIT

First issued to mechanics and tank crewmen during June 1940, the loose-fitting coverall, later dubbed the 'jungle suit', was designed to fit over the service uniform. It had two square-flapped breast pockets without buttons, the left hand pocket sometimes bearing the stencilled Marine emblem and acronym 'USMC'. In the lower rear were two open patch pockets, the right hand pocket having a narrow extension to accommodate a wrench or ruler. Both the cuffs and trousers bottoms were secured by tabs and a single steel Marine Corps-marked button. The full front fly was fastened by seven buttons of the same pattern. An opening either side at waist-level provided access to inner garments.

Mainly issued to Marine artillery personnel and support units, the jungle suit was often worn unbuttoned with the top half rolled down, and had to be completely removed when nature called! General R. L. Eichelberger was well aware of the misery of the troops in coveralls facing the Japanese perimeter at Buna on New Guinea in early 1943. For countless weeks, he recalled, 'no-one could remember when he had last been dry.

The feet, arms, stomachs, chests, armpits of my soldiers were hideous with jungle rot. The sun appeared when the skies wrung themselves out briefly, and steam rose like grey smoke in the dark undergrowth. Then the soldiers themselves steamed and sweated in their heavy jungle suits.' Nonetheless, Marine paratroops later preferred the one-piece garment, which did not separate when jumping.

The introduction of two-piece 'utilities' marks a turning point in the development of Marine Corps uniform. Combining fatigue and field service clothing, which was ideally suited to the warm climate of the Pacific Theatre of World War Two, Marines still wear a version of the utility uniform for field service today. The 1941-pattern, herringbone twill, sage green utility uniform was first approved for issue on the Marine Corps' birthday, 11 November 1941, and consisted of a sack-type coat, which Marines often referred to as a 'jacket', and trousers. The coat was clearly based

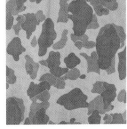

Left, **coat worn with the two-piece camouflage uniform issued from mid-1943.**

Above, **detail showing 'frog' pattern camouflage green side and brown side.** *Photos by the author, courtesy of Jim Moran*

This Marine wears the pre-war sun helmet together with his newly-issued two-piece utility uniform. He holds the old 1903 Springfield with 1908 pattern long bayonet fixed. *NA 127-N-515695*

on the blue denim pattern it was designed to replace. Loose-fitting, it was fastened down the front with four two-piece buttons bearing the inscription 'U.S. MARINE CORPS' in raised letters. The cuffs were closed by a single button of the same pattern, which could be passed through a choice of two button holes for adjustment. A single patch pocket was sewn to the left breast, on which was stencilled in black ink the letters 'USMC' over the 1936-pattern Marine Corps 'eagle, globe, and anchor' emblem. A row of stitching about 1½ inches from the pocket inner edge formed a pen pocket. Two larger patch pockets were attached to the front coat skirts. The trousers were straight-legged and cuffless, with belt loops and covered front fly which was fastened by five metal Marine Corps buttons. They had two internally-hung front pockets with slash openings, the right hand one having a small watch pocket, and two rear patch pockets. A later pattern dispensed with the watch pocket.

The buttons on both the coat and trousers were originally copper-plated, but an emergency alternative specification was approved on 15 August 1942 which required the button to be 'parkerized, bonderized or oxidized... and coated with a phrenol formaldehyde baked on coating pigment to produce as near as possible a novelty bronze shade'.

When first issued, the coat was stamped with the maker's name in indelible ink on the inside behind the breast pocket. The trousers were marked in the same fashion on the waistband or under the right front pocket. These markings usually vanished after several washes. Marines often personalised their coats by either stencilling or writing their names on or over the breast pocket, on one of the lower hip pockets, or even across the back of the coat, inside or out.

From 1943, a short-visored, sage green, herringbone twill, utility cap, inspired by railroad worker's headgear, appears to have been issued, with and without the Marine Corps emblem stencilled on the front, or sometimes with a small metal Marine Corps emblem attached to the headband or visor. This cap proved to be very popular with Marines, who often wore it underneath, and sometimes in place of, the M1 helmet! A utility hat of the same material, with soft floppy brim, had also been available since 1936.

M1 HELMET

The M1 helmet, with its original fibre liner, was adopted by American forces on 9 June 1941, after much experimentation by the US Army Board. Produced by the McCord Radiator and Manufacturing Company, and made of Hadfield manganese steel, the olive drab-painted outer helmet was designed to cover as much of the head as possible, without impeding the wearer's vision or restricting his actions. Also incorporated was a visor at the front, and slight outward swell at the sides and back of the helmet, to prevent rain from running down the wearer's neck. After its initial issuance, the M1 helmet was found to have a magnetic influence on compass readings. An attempt to rectify this was made by edging the helmet with non-magnetic stainless steel. This was subsequently changed to another metal because the stainless steel reflected sunlight when the paint chipped off.

The first pattern M1 helmet liners were made by the Hawley Products Company, and were constructed of the same material as the pre-war sun helmet. This consisted of two rigid, water resistant, fibre shells which were cemented together and covered with olive drab twill. An adjustable rayon webbing suspension system was attached inside the liner. A soft leather chinstrap, with small open-frame buckle, could be worn under the chin when wearing the liner only. When both steel shell and liner were donned, this strap was usually fastened over the front visor.

Considered too heavy, rather fragile and easily crushed, the fibre liner was only ever intended as

a stop-gap measure until a better product could be developed. Nonetheless, about four million of this type were purchased for US forces. In February 1942, the fibre liner began to be replaced by a new model, described in quartermaster catalogues as plastic linen, composed of phenol-formaldehyde resin impregnated, lightweight, duck cloth which was laminated under high-pressure. Both sorts of helmet liners were worn by the Marine Corps throughout the war.

Based on photographic evidence, it is apparent that from 1943 the Marine Corps used a series of tactical markings which were usually stencilled on either the back, or right breast, of the utility coat, and sometimes on the helmet cover. An outer symbol such as a diamond, a rectangle, or a circle, indicated the division. Within this was usually to be found a three-digit code number, the first digit indicating the unit within the division, the second referring to the actual battalion, and the last signifying the company within the battalion. As regulation rank insignia was not officially permitted to be worn on the 'utility' uniform, some units appear to have added a number above the unit code, either inside or outside the divisional symbol, which represented rank, for example, ' 1' – Private First Class, '2' – corporal, '3' – sergeant, '4' – lieutenant, '5' – captain, '6' – major and above. According to Captain J. Fred Haley, '...the officers and non-commissioned officers in the 8th Marines had their insignia of rank painted on the cloth camouflage cover... worn over the steel helmet. This was done with dull, black ink, and the result was difficult to see except when the observer was close at hand.' Photographic evidence, plus surviving uniforms, indicates that NCOs also painted non-regulation chevrons on their coat sleeves.

The 1941 pattern utility uniform, and M1 helmet and liner, commonly known among Marines as the 'bucket', was issued to the flood of Marine Corps recruits during the early months of 1942, and first saw large scale service on the beaches of

Right from top to bottom; The fibre sun helmet, worn by the Marine Corps in tropical climates until 1941. Note the ventilation holes and 'turban' pattern sewn into the crown. The M-1917A1 steel helmet, or 'dishpan', was basically a refurbished World War One M-1917 helmet. Although against regulations, the front has been drilled or punched to accommodate the bronze service cap emblem; detail showing new leather head-lining. Note the webbing chin-strap, which is fixed to the lining, has also been passed through the original, now redundant, WW1 metal loops attached to the helmet. The M1 helmet with second pattern herringbone twill camouflage cover showing 'green' side out; interior of M1 helmet showing liner and rayon webbing suspension system. *Photos by the author, courtesy of Jim Moran*

THE MARINES HAVE LANDED—!

APPLY TO NEAREST RECRUITING STATION

Guadalcanal in August of that year. However, stateside contractors could not keep up with demand for service wear, and by the end of the year a shortage had become apparent. As a consequence, the men of the exhausted 1st Marine Division sent from Guadalcanal to Australia to re-fit on 9 December 1942 received a temporary issue of Australian-made khaki 'battle jackets', or blouses, which closely resembled British Army battle dress, but with buttoned cuff tabs and collar pressed open for wear with collar and tie.

Where available, the Marine Corps utility uniform remained unchanged until after the landings at Tarawa in the Gilbert Islands on 20-21 November 1943. During this operation, Colonel David M. Shoup, who led the 2nd Marines ashore, observed that too many men hit the beach with only their rifles, having jettisoned most of their accoutrements and cartridge belts when they jumped into the deep water from their landing craft. After the Gilberts operation, Shoup ordered Corporal Andrew J. Marcinko, a company-tailor in his regiment, to design a modified uniform with sufficient cargo pockets to enable each Marine to carry ammunition, rations, and a poncho during future landings. Corporal Marcinko set to work and came up with a completely new utility uniform.

Once again made of herringbone twill, the new coat was fastened by six buttons of the same pattern as used previously, and had a gas flap composed of a strip of material which fastened on the inside front to form a second seal when the garment was buttoned up. The left hand breast pocket with Marine Corps stencil was retained, but was placed higher up and had a square top flap added, which closed with a single button. In place of the two lower skirt pockets, the new coat had two deep inside breast pockets for maps and grenades. Besides the two front slash pockets, the new trousers had large flapped 'grenade' pockets at each thigh, within which a box of K-rations fitted perfectly. In place of the hip pockets, these trousers had a flapped bellows pocket measuring nine by eleven inches across the seat. Secured by three buttons, it was designed to carry the camouflaged poncho, although many Marines preferred to loop the latter over the back of their cartridge belt, and kept socks and other necessities in their 'butt' pocket. Besides belt loops, the trouser waist band also had eyelets for attaching webbing suspenders, while the leg cuffs had further eyelets for drawstrings. Known subsequently as 1944-pattern 'modified' utilities, this uniform saw little combat service during World War Two.

CAMOUFLAGE

The need for camouflage uniforms on the beaches and in the jungles of the Pacific Islands quickly became apparent, and some Marine units, especially the elite Raider battalions, began to daub their 1941 pattern utility uniforms with green and brown paint. These units also dyed their utilities black for night operations. Some early-issue plain coveralls were rendered even more uncomfortable when officers ordered them to be 'dyed a mottled green to aid concealment', and the dye closed all the breathing holes in the herringbone twill cloth.

Opposite, this recruiting poster, featuring a painting by James Montgomery Flagg, illustrates the Marines as they looked at the beginning of the Pacific War in 1941. They wear the summer service uniform complete with M-1917A1 steel helmets. *Peter Newark's Military Pictures*

Above, the men featured in this 1942 poster for the documentary film 'We are the Marines' wear newly issued M1 helmets and utility uniforms. *Peter Newark's Military Pictures*

The US Army had already begun to test numerous types of camouflage during 1940, and eventually adopted a distinctive pattern. Produced in two colour combinations for reversible uniforms, the 'green side', consisting of light and dark green and brown spots on a pale green background, was designed for use in the jungle; the 'brown side', with dark, medium and light brown spots on a khaki backgound, was for use on the beaches. In the field it made little difference which 'side out' was worn, although the green combination appears to have seen the most use.

The Marines received the first issue camouflage clothing during 1943, which consisted of a modified version of the Army-pattern herringbone twill one-piece coverall, or jungle suit. A reversible garment using the green and brown camouflage patterns, it had pleated breast pockets with flaps fastened by two, olive drab-painted press studs, or 'glove snaps', and cargo pockets of the same type on the front thighs. The wrist cuffs were secured by a tab which buttoned to a single Army-type, black metal, '13 star' button. Leg cuffs were plain. The 'bi-swing' back had two pleats running from shoulder to waist. Internal suspenders, or braces, with slide adjusters, were added to assist with weight distribution when the front cargo pockets were full. In practice these were seldom used,

and often removed, because they cut into the wearer's shoulders. Mainly issued to artillery and service troops, the jungle suit caused the wearer the same problems as the one-piece mechanic's coveralls. They were too hot, became too heavy when wet, and were impractical when it came to a call of nature, although many men cut 'butt' flaps into them to relieve the latter problem!

Although camouflage coveralls continued to see use until at least 1944, the Marine Corps received its own two-piece camouflage uniform during mid-1943. Initially supplied on only a limited basis to 'elite troops' such as Raiders and scout snipers, by November of that year it was generally available to larger infantry units. Cut in the same pattern as the 1941 utilities, it used the same reversible camouflage pattern as found on the jungle suit. Besides the left breast pocket marked with the Marine Corps stencil, the coat had only one skirt pocket, usually on the right hand side. It was fastened by five black metal glove snaps, four of which were spaced up the front from waist to throat, and the fifth offset at the throat to secure the collar. Cuffs were plain without fasteners or tabs.

The accompanying trousers were fastened by four outside glove snaps which did not stand up well to field wear. The single front and rear patch pockets were also unpopular, and according to Rudy Rosenquist who served in the 3rd Raider Battalion, many Raiders cut through to gain additional access to the inner pockets on the 'brown' side.

The 1944-pattern, modified two-piece camouflage uniform overcame many of the above shortcomings. Possibly intended only for Marine Parachute battalions, but not made available in quantity until after the disbandment of those units, it first saw service on Saipan in June 1944. On this version, the glove snaps were replaced by four black metal 'US Marine Corps' buttons, which also fastened its adjustable cuffs. The patch pockets

This photo of Colonel David Shoup's command post on Tarawa in November, 1943 illustrates how utility clothing and M1 helmets were mixed in the field. The two men at right wear camouflage coats 'green' side out with plain sage green trousers. Three men are without helmet covers, while the man seated in the foreground, the legendary Raider, Lieutenant Colonel Evans Carlson, wears the **sniper's helmet cover with integral cotton band around its base to accommodate foliage. Note also the officer at centre, wears collar bars, a most unusual sight in combat. The officer to his right with the M1928 document case over his shoulder is Colonel Shoup, while Colonel Merrit A. Edson, commander of the 1st Raider Battalion, stands in the rear left with hands on hips. *NA 127-N-63505***

Left, Marines manning a 75 mm pack howitzer pass ammunition to the gun crew as they blast away at the Japanese positions on Cape Gloucester airfield during December 1943. They all wear US Army issue M1942 one-piece camouflage coveralls with Marine 1936-pattern round, herringbone twill, fatigue hats.
Imperial War Museum Photo # NYF 16923

Below, men of the 2nd Battalion, 24th Marines being interviewed by combat radio correspondent Sergeant Richard Mawson behind the front lines on Iwo Jima during February 1945. These Marines wear both types of camouflage covers on their helmets. Two men wear camouflage ponchos.
NA 127-N-112637

were replaced by two large internal chest pockets with vertical access each side of the front closure. These were each secured by a single glove snap. Two slightly different patterns of trousers were worn with this coat. Both had an exposed five-button fly, waistband eyelets to accommodate the 1941 pack suspenders, front internal pockets and a large 'butt' pocket.

The first helmet camouflage worn by the Marine Corps was developed early in the war by the Raider Battalions who began to cover their helmets with burlap, to which was sewn strips of herringbone twill daubed with olive drab paint. Production helmet covers began to appear in 1943 with the camouflage two-piece utility uniform. They were made of the same herringbone twill cloth as the uniform, and were printed with the same reversible camouflage patterns. The cover fitted to the helmet by means of six flaps which tucked up inside the steel shell when it was replaced over the liner. The two rear flaps were often left hanging loose to protect the wearer's neck from sunburn.

A second pattern helmet cover was introduced in late 1943 or early 1944. Identical in construction to the first pattern, it also had two rows of small horizontal, hem stitched slits spaced around the sides for the attachment of additional camouflage. A third pattern or 'sniper' helmet cover also appeared during 1943. Made from lightweight cotton cloth, it was non-reversible, bearing the 'green' camouflage colours on both sides. It also had a green cotton band around the base of the skull, which was sewn down at intervals to form loops for foliage attachment. In addition, it had attached to the bottom edge an integral face veil of camouflage printed mosquito netting, which could be tied by means of tapes around the wearer's neck or shoulders.

Other camouflage items issued to the Marine Corps by 1943 included a reversible half shelter, or 'pup', tent which was shared between two Marines, and a reversible waterproofed light cotton poncho. Both of these items had been available in olive drab before that date.

During their brief existence, the elite Marine Parachute troops, or 'Paramarines', were issued a variety of specialist clothing. On organisation in 1941, the first units received a sage green, herringbone twill garment modelled on the German paratrooper, or *Fallschirmjager*, smock. Designed to be worn over the mechanic's coveralls, it was one-piece with short integral legs reaching to mid-thigh and throat-to-crotch front zipper. External impact pads of horsehide covered with tan canvas protected the elbows. On each side of the lower hip was a large external pocket, again covered with tan canvas, which closed at the top by a horizontal zipper, although a variant pattern had flaps fastened down by three snaps. These probably had horsehide inserts which could be removed after a jump, thereby serving as cargo pockets. On the left breast was a small bellows pocket secured by two 'glove snaps', with 'USMC' stencilled on the flap and the Corps emblem on the smock front above it. The right breast pocket was larger with three snaps. A large flapped pocket was also attached to the upper part of the pleated, or 'bi-swing', back.

With the general introduction of camouflage clothing during late 1942 or early 1943, Marine paratroopers received a reversible camouflage smock. Probably never used in combat, it was also of step-in design, being fastened by six plain snaps, but retaining the horsehide elbow pads which in this case were sewn internally. On each breast was a flapped pocket, set 30 degrees to the vertical, and on either lower hip a large, horizontal, flapped pocket. All four pockets were closed by three glove snaps. A large internal cargo pocket, accessed either end by a flapped and zipped opening again set 30 degrees to the vertical, was let into the back.

The costly production of the camouflage smock led to the production in 1943 of a simplified, third pattern parachutist's camouflage smock, which had externally sewn elbow pads, and breast pockets

Opposite, **Private First Class, 3rd Marine Division, 1943. During the savage and costly counter-offensive against the Japanese in the Pacific, the Marines fully established their reputation as an élite fighting force. The subject here is a Private, First Class, of the 3rd Marine Division as he would have appeared on Bougainville during February 1943. He wears model 1941 'utilities' or 'dungarees', in 'olive drab' herringbone twill cotton, which quickly faded to a pale grey-green. His standard MI** steel helmet is covered with a cloth camouflage cover peculiar to the Marines. Like other camouflaged gear worn by the Corps, it was brown on one side, and mainly green on the other, being theoretically reversible for operations on the beaches or in jungle. Over his shoulder is an Army-issue M4 satchel containing an M6 gasmask, plus an ammunition bandolier, a throw-away item issued ready-packed with 12 clips for his rifle. A hand grenade, Mk.II defensive, is attached to his adjustable canvas suspenders. He wears web leggings and standard-issue 'boondocker' shoes with rubber heels and soles. He is holding an M1 Garand, the semi-automatic rifle carried by most Marine riflemen by 1943, attached to which is a M1907 khaki-coloured woven sling with steel fittings. He is surrounded by weapons and equipment: (top) M1 carbine; (top right) a haversack, closed and open; (middle right) model 1941 Pack System, complete with camouflage, shelter half poncho and entrenching tool; (lower right) first pattern 'cross flap' canteen cover and aluminium canteen; M1 bayonet with black plastic grip, and M7 plastic scabbard; 'K-Bar' knife and sheath; (bottom right) pattern-1936 canvas leggings; (top left) bronzed button with raised 'U.S. Marine Corps' legend; (upper left) M1 Garand rifle; (lower left) model 1928 rifle belt with equipment suspenders; (bottom left) First aid dressing and pouch. *Painting by Richard Hook*

SMALL
FIRST-AID DRESSING
U.S. ARMY

which resembled the second pattern USMC two-piece utilities.

A two-piece, Marine parachutist's reversible camouflage uniform, possibly designed to wear under the camouflage smock which was presumably to be discarded after the jump, was worn by the Paramarines in the Solomon Islands and later. Early versions were produced in canvas of shelter-half weight, but subsequent production returned to the use of herringbone twill. The loose-fitting coat was closed by six glove snaps, and the two angled breast pockets were secured by means of a single snap. The trousers had internal flapless front pockets on the 'green' side, while on the 'brown' side they appeared as patch pockets with a flap and three snaps. In the rear was a large 'butt' pocket which hung externally on the 'green' side and internally on the 'brown' side. Access was facilitated either side by means of slanted, flapped openings at either end.

A forest green woollen helmet was used during training jumps at the beginning of the Pacific War. This was superseded in early 1942 by a helmet made of dark brown goatskin with a chamois leather lining, which could be worn with or without the M1 helmet and liner during jumps. A chrome buckle at either side of the chin of the leather jump helmet facilitated the attachment of a chin-strap or

cup. Leather loops were sewn to its sides and rear, through which goggle straps could be passed. A small number of the Army-pattern M2 parachutist's steel helmets with liners containing extra webbing and chin-cups, plus camouflage covers, were also issued to the Paramarines during 1942.

Marine tank crews wore a moulded, highly compressed cardboard composite and leather helmet. Painted olive drab, it had large ventilation holes across the top, and separate ear-flaps, plus a nape flap, for protection. Riveted sprung straps fixed either side held earphones close to the ears. Early war models of this helmet had a large padded ring running around the brim which provided the wearer with protection inside the tank. This feature was abandoned during late 1941 or early 1942, to enable a standard M1 steel helmet outer shell to be worn over the top when desirable.

SPRINGFIELD RIFLE

The main infantry small arm carried by the Marines at the beginning of the Pacific War was the single-shot, clip-fed, .30-calibre M1903 Springfield rifle, of which 52,000 were serviceable and in the hands of the Corps prior to Pearl Harbor. The M1903A1 rifle had been standardised in 1929, but was not mass produced until 1939. The M1905 bayonet, measuring $20\frac{1}{2}$ inches in length, inclusive of a 16-inch blade, was attached to this weapon at the beginning of the war. Manufactured at the Springfield Armory and Rock Island Arsenal, it had a walnut grip and fitted into the M1910 khaki canvas-covered scabbard with leather tip, which fastened to the rifle belt via two wire hooks attached to the back of the metal throat.

The demands of wartime quickly exhausted supplies of both the M1905 bayonet and accompanying scabbard. Hence a new and less well-made version of this bayonet was mass produced from 1942 onwards which consisted basically of the 1905 metalwork with a black, or occasionally brown, plastic grip. Regarding

Above, At the beginning of the Pacific war, the Marine carried the M1903 'Springfield' rifle, calibre .30-06, which was a bolt action weapon capable of firing either a single round or a five-round clip. The model seen here was manufactured at the Springfield Armory. *Courtesy of Jim Moran, photo by the author*

Top, detail showing the five round clip being loaded. The serial number on the breech indicates that this particular weapon was made during February, 1920. *Courtesy of Jim Moran, photo by the author*

scabbards, the compatible, green painted leather, M1917 Enfield scabbard was adopted and issued as an interim measure. Furthermore, contracts were issued for the production of new M1910 canvas-covered scabbards. Meanwhile, on 17 November 1941 the Beckworth Manufacturing Company and the Detroit Gasket & Manufacturing Company were given contracts to mass produce a new model, made from a composite plastic material with a metal throat, which was eventually classified as the M3 bayonet scabbard.

Although giving good service, the long blade on the M1905 bayonet generated criticism in some quarters during the early part of World War Two.

The most common complaint was that the 16-inch blade was inconvenient and cumbersome for troops travelling in modern vehicles and transport vessels. Also, a perceived reduction in bayonet fighting lessened the need for a long-bladed bayonet. Thus a bayonet similar to the M1905, but with an overall length of only 14 inches and a shorter 10-inch blade, was under development during 1942. Initially, a number of M1905s with shortened 10-inch blades were successfully field tested and subsequently classified as M1905E1 bayonets. This ultimately led to the mass production, from April 1943, of the shorter M1 bayonet with either black or brown plastic grip.

Left, a late-1944 production, calibre .30, M1 Rifle made at the Springfield Armory. Designed by John C. Garand, this semi-automatic weapon which took an 8-round clip was adopted by the Marine Corps in 1943 after extensive trials.
Courtesy of Jim Moran, photo by the author

Above, Marines of the 2nd Division prepare to take a Japanese block-house on Tarawa in November 1943. The man in the foreground holds an M1 carbine plus a belt of .30 calibre ammunition, and wears his helmet reversed, possibly to improve his vision. The man in the rear is about to toss a hand grenade.
Imperial War Museum Photo # NYF 11285

A total of 2,948,649 M1 bayonets were produced before the end of the war, while about one million M1905s were shortened. The plastic M7 scabbard, which was basically a shorter version of the M3, was also adopted to accommodate this bayonet. At the same time M3 scabbards were shortened for the same purpose, being classified as the M7 scabbard.

Regarding the development of the Springfield rifle, an updated M1903A3 was also adopted in 1942. Marine snipers continued to prefer the original M1903 with a Layman No. 5A 5x telescope, or the 'special reference' M1903A1 with Unertl 8x target scope. A bolt action weapon using a five-round magazine, the '03 Springfield' was briefly retained in use after the introduction of the M1 Garand rifle, with an M1 rifle grenade launcher attached, on the ratio of one per squad.

Another semi-automatic weapon, the .30-calibre, ten-shot, rotary magazine M1941 Johnson rifle, designed by Captain Melvin Johnson, a Marine Reservist, saw limited service in Marine hands before the Garand took over in large numbers.

Above, **an M1 carbine made by the Inland Manufacturing Division of General Motors, at Dayton, Ohio, in May 1944. Improved features on this late-war weapon include the T4 barrel band with bayonet lug, and adjustable rear sight. Note the magazine pouch attached to the stock.** *Courtesy of Jim Moran, photo by the author*

Top, **detail showing the 15-round magazine being loaded.** *Courtesy of Jim Moran, photo by the author*

GARAND RIFLE

The Marine Corps first officially received the Army's semi-automatic, 8-round, 30-calibre M1 Garand rifle, designed by John C. Garand, during April 1943, after it had left Guadalcanal and was in Australia training for the impending New Britain operation. This weapon weighed 11 1⁄4 lbs including a full magazine, sling, and oiler bottle in the stock. Many 'old time' Leathernecks distrusted the new weapon. When the last round had been fired, the clip would eject rather noisily, which indicated to any one within earshot that the rifle was empty! Others doubted its accuracy, or believed it was too complex for new recruits to use. Nonetheless, the full worth of the M1 quickly became apparent in the field, and it was unofficially acquired by some Marines through bartering, or 'moonlight requisition', after the Army had arrived on Guadalcanal during October 1942. Others obtained them by commandeering the weapons left by those soldiers who had been wounded and evacuated. The popularity of the fast-firing M1 Garand over the slower and more laborious '03 Springfield may be judged by the observed actions of one Marine who participated in a joint operation with Army personnel on Guadalcanal: 'I saw this Marine, a member of the 2nd Raider Battalion, place and keep himself squarely behind one of the army sergeants in the advance platoon. When the march was well underway the sergeant inquired as to why the leatherneck kept treading on his heels. The answer came quickly; "You'll probably get yours on the first burst, Mac! Before you hit the ground I'll throw this damn Springfield away and grab your rifle." Phased in on a regimental basis, most Marines were officially in receipt of the M1 Garand by the end of 1943.

The M1 carbine was adopted by the Marine Corps during January 1942. More compact than a rifle but with greater fire-power than a pistol, this light-weight, 5.5 lb, .30-calibre semi-automatic weapon usually carried a 15-round magazine.

A small number of folding stock M1A1 carbines were issued to Paramarine units during the same year, while by 1945 the fully automatic M2 carbine was in the hands of some Marine units. The carbine was never intended to replace the M1 rifle. Indeed, one official Marine Corps report stated: 'On Saipan the M1 [rifle] continued as an excellent weapon, more durable than the carbine, and, although much heavier, it was preferred by most Marines. A carbine bullet would not always stop an enemy soldier.'

MACHINE GUNS

The .45-calibre Thompson sub-machine gun had been carried by the Marines since 1922, but saw only limited service during the Pacific War. In fact, only 10,000 were required by the Marine Corps in January 1942, for issue purely to divisional scout and military police units, and to the Raiders. The M1928A1 used a 50-round drum at the beginning of the war, but subsequently either 20-round or 30-round stick magazines were issued. The improved M1, made available in 1942, took either a 30-round box magazine or the 20-rounder. Ill-suited to frontline use as they sounded too much like Japanese 6.5 mm light machine guns, the 'Tommy gun' was generally withdrawn from US service in April 1944.

The Reising .45-calibre M50 and M55 sub-

A Marine armed with a .30-calibre Browning M1919A4 machine gun lies deep in the underbrush on New Britain Island, full equipment beside him and 'K-Bar' knife on his belt. *Imperial War Museum Photo # NYF 14623*

machine gun was an even more controversial weapon. Adopted in 1940, approximately 4,200 were authorised per Marine Division, with about 500 being originally assigned to each regiment. The M50 had a full wood stock and weighed 6.75 lbs, while the slightly lighter M55, fitted with a folding wire stock and minus muzzle compensator, was used by the Raiders and Paramarines. Both weapons used a 20-round magazine, and both were prone to jamming or misfiring. Captain G. L. H. Cooper, who commanded an engineer company on Guadalcanal in 1942, recalled: 'It seems that company grade officers, such as myself, were armed at this time with a thing called a Reising gun — sort of a poor man's Thompson submachine gun. It wasn't a bad looking contraption, but closer inspection showed that most of its components had been stamped rather than machined. It had a bad habit of firing full automatic when selected for semi-automatic, or for that matter, when the safety switch was on. Aiming required Kentucky windage strictly out of this world, and the bluing left a lot to be desired, particularly in a place such as Guadalcanal where rust, mildew and general rot got at the best equipment. Altogether, it wasn't a very satisfactory weapon and could be highly dangerous — to the shooter and not the shootee, that is. Therefore, it should be understandable that most of us wanted to get rid of this undesirable piece of impedimenta.' Captain Cooper 'exchanged' his Reising machine gun for a Colt .45 pistol soon after, and most Reisings had been withdrawn from service by the end of 1942.

Pump-action shotguns, such as the Winchester 12-gauge M1897 and M1912, had become popular among Marines during the 'Banana Wars' earlier in the century. Not officially issued in the Pacific until April 1943, each regiment was authorised 100 of this weapon type, which had a 20-inch barrel, a six-round tubular magazine, and perforated barrel hand guard. The shotgun was very effective in clearing out Japanese bunkers and trenches.

Left, **M1905 bayonet and M3 plastic scabbard. This bayonet was manufactured by the Springfield Armory in 1917.**
Courtesy of the Ministry of Defence Pattern Room photos by the author

Above, **Private Mantuano adjusts his 1941 pack system in its Transport Pack combination. Although this photograph was taken at the San Diego recruiting depot in 1943, he still wears the fibre sun helmet.**
NA 127-N-41745

Fundamental to the Marine rifle squad's armoury was the .30-calibre M1918, M1918A1 and M1918A2 Browning automatic rifle (BAR), which had a fire rate of 300 to 400 rounds per minute using 20-round box magazines. Although cumbersome compared with the M1 Garand rifle, and weighing 19.4 lbs, the number of BARs per squad had been increased from one to four by the end of the war. The original M1918 BAR, and some A1s with a bipod near the muzzle, had a wooden butt. By 1942, all A1 and A2 models had a plastic butt, while a carrying handle was introduced in 1943. The later A2 model had an upgraded rear sight, and selective high and low rates of fire.

The Paramarines used the Johnson .30-calibre M1941 light machine gun as a squad automatic weapon. Similar in capability to the BAR, it had a curved 20-round magazine, selective fire facility, and weighed only 13 lbs. Like its rifle counterpart, it saw only limited service in World War Two.

Since 1912, the Colt .45-calibre M1911 and M1911A1 pistol, with seven-round magazine, had been the standard Marine Corps side arm. This weapon was largely replaced by the M1 carbine in both infantry and artillery regiments after April 1943, although many Marines continued to carry their 'forty-five automatics'.

After basic training, or Boot Camp, every enlisted Marine on service in the Pacific from 1941 to 1945 was issued with standard '782 gear', which consisted of a full set of field equipment, all of which was recorded on Form 782. Used as a receipt, this document was returned to the Marine on release from the Corps once he had returned each item of equipment.

Fundamental to the '782' gear of the Marine was the canvas web belt. Riflemen wore the M1928 rifle belt which had ten pouches, each of which could hold either two 5-round '03 chargers or one 8-round M1 clip. Earlier versions of this belt featured brass hardware, and had a dividing strap that fastened by a snap in each pouch. Many M1928

belts issued to the Marines were stamped inside with 'U.S.M.C.' plus the name of the maker and year of production. In its originally issued form, the colour of this belt ranged from olive drab to khaki, but usually ended by being bleached in salt water and the Pacific sun to a creamy off-white colour, which Marines termed 'salty'. The whiter the webbing, the 'saltier' the Marine.

A number of weapons and accoutrements were customarily attached to the rifle belt via hooks through belt eyelets. Weapons included both the M1905 and M1 bayonet and scabbard, utility knife, machete, bolo, trench knife, and, in the case of Raiders, the 'Gung Ho' and stiletto knives. Standard accoutrements included the first aid dressing pouch, jungle first aid pouch from 1944 onwards, and canteen in canvas cover.

Officers and other personnel, such as Military Police, wore the canvas web M1936 pistol belt which had a maximum of 16 pairs of evenly-spaced eyelets to facilitate the carriage of a holstered pistol, canteen, first aid dressing pouch, compass pouch, plus a variety of ammunition pouches for automatic and semi-automatic weapons. Pistols were also carried in the issue M4 shoulder holster, although many men acquired holsters which were privately purchased.

Marines armed with the M1 carbine attached the larger carbine clip pouches to the pistol belt. The Browning automatic rifle operator and his assistant wore the canvas web M1918 BAR belt, or later M1937 variant. The belt worn by the former had four BAR magazine pouches, a metal cup to hold the butt steady while firing when standing, plus a pouch for two pistol magazines for his sidearm. The latter usually employed four BAR magazine pouches and four rifle clip pouches.

Prior to Pearl Harbor, the Marine Corps adopted the M1941 pack system, which replaced the M1928 and even older M1910 haversacks. The M1941 system

Right from top to bottom; **World War II production M1 bayonet; M1905 bayonet modified to M1 configuration with clipped point blade. Note the difference in the blade fullers between the two types of bayonet; M7 scabbard. The Marine '1219C2 utility knife', issued from 1943 and still used today.**

This example is the KA-BAR produced by the Union Cutlery Company. The most commonly used, all other types were subsequently named 'K-Bar' knives. M4 Bayonet-Knife and M8A1 scabbard. *Courtesy of the Ministry of Defence Pattern Room/Jim Moran, photos by the author*

comprised a top haversack, a bottom knapsack, and a set of adjustable, load bearing suspenders. The haversack consisted of a back pack made of heavy tan duck canvas, with top flap and 'ears' which tucked underneath when the pack was closed. By means of straps and eyelets, an entrenching tool could be attached to the front of the haversack, while a scabbarded bayonet or machete could be secured to its left side. The knapsack, of similar design, was attached to the bottom of the haversack via a heavy canvas strap. When fully assembled with long blanket roll consisting of shelter half and two blankets secured around it, this combination was called the Field Transport Pack. Haversack and knapsack without blanket roll, usually worn in transit where bivouac items were not required, was classified as the Transport Pack. The haversack worn on its own was known as the Light Marching Pack, and as the Field Marching Pack with short blanket roll attached. Marines usually went into combat wearing the latter combination at the beginning of the Pacific War.

Marine officers and personnel who were unable to carry the M1941 pack system, such as heavy weapons teams and tank crews, were issued a M1936 single canvas field bag, or 'musette', with a central divider designed to separate the mess kit and rations from other contents. By means of adjustable straps, this bag could be worn either on the back or slung at the hip.

Although the Marine Corps continued to take pride in its prowess as riflemen during the Pacific War, its expanding role in combat ensured that it fought with a variety of heavier weaponry. Prior to Pearl Harbor, the standard crew-served light machine gun had been the Navy .30-calibre Lewis, Mk. 6 Model 1. Mounted on a bipod, this 27 lb weapon with its 47-round pan magazine gave good service in the Philippines during the early stages of the war. Similarly, the slightly heavier .30-calibre Browning M1919A4 was extremely reliable, being

issued to rifle company weapons platoons as the conflict progressed.

For long-range fire support, the Marine Corps used the the water-cooled, tripod-mounted, .30-calibre M1917A1 heavy machine gun which was initially issued to battalion weapons companies, but was later deployed among rifle company weapons platoons when the former were discarded in 1944. On Saipan, PFC Jeremiah Hanafin, 3rd Battalion, 6th Marines, experienced problems as second gunner: 'The heavy machine gun had a correspondingly heavy tripod... once down valuable time was spent spreading the legs and adjusting them. With the light tripod you just threw it down and clamped on the gun. The assault waves [on Saipan] tried a compromise approach: light tripods with heavy guns. This allowed for quicker mobility and ease in setting up. Once a stable perimeter had been established the heavy tripods would be brought in. Problem was, the heavy guns really jumped when fired on the light tripods.'

Also water-cooled were the .50-calibre M1912A1 and M2 anti-aircraft machine guns, which used either 110-round metallic link belts or a 500-round container. Marines generally manned '.50-cals' on troop-carrying ships aswell as in ground defence positions.

BIG GUNS

Another effective ground fire support weapon was the 81 mm M1 mortar, which was used at battalion level, while the 60 mm M2 mortar was employed on a company basis. Capable of being transported on the M6A1 hand-cart, both of these weapons gave Marines good service throughout the war. PFC Thomas M. Hanafin had mixed feelings about his experience with mortars: 'I wanted to be a rifleman, but they assigned me to the 81 mm mortars. If I remember correctly there were eight men, or more, to a squad, and each had to learn everyone else's job. I didn't like the mortars, but then I had no choice. I stayed with them all through my training

Previous page, the quick-firing Bofors 40 mm M1 anti-aircraft gun was often used as a ground attack weapon. These Marines on Bougainville in 1943 are firing their weapon at close range over open sights. *Imperial War Museum Photo # HU 75665*

on British Samoa. The thing that most of us dreaded was a misfire... In that case, one man would tip the tube very carefully while another cupped his hands over the mouth and caught the shell as it slid out. You had to make sure you didn't touch the detonator, or it was good-bye. One day, as we were firing out on the range, we heard, "Misfire!" The sergeant walked up to the two men who were on the mortar and said, "You know what to do." The whole squad just got up and walked away. To this day I don't know who took the shell out of the tube.'

The portable flamethrower was especially effective in reducing Japanese bunkers and strong-points. First employed as an offensive weapon by Marines on Guadalcanal in January 1943, the M1 flamethrower had only a 15-yard range, but by the following July the M1A1 model, with thicker fuel and 50-yard range, was in service. By July 1944, the M2-2 flamethrower with a 60-yard range was in use on Guam. After dealing with a Jap bomb shelter on Tarawa with his M1A1 in 1943, PFC Robert Harper recalled: 'They were huddled in there scared to death. I turned on the heat and that was all'.

Included among the anti-aircraft weapons served by the Marines at sea was the 60-round magazine-fed, fully automatic Oerlikon 20 mm Mk 4 gun.

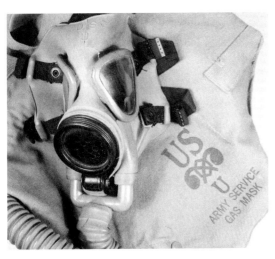

Left, the Army service gas mask was standard issue to all Marines until 1944, after which the Corps adopted a lightweight gas mask with olive green rubber face piece carried in an olive drab haversack. Seen here is the M3-1XA-1VA1 gas mask which had an integral diaphragm which enabled speech to be heard. Issuance was officially restricted to telephone operators, officers and enlisted men performing duties which necessitated giving orders, and personnel performing fire control duties. Gas masks were often the first piece of equipment to be discarded after a beach assault in the Pacific. *Photo by the author, courtesy of Jim Moran*

Above, sadly, burial detail was one of the few occasions when the gas mask proved useful. Two of the Marines seen here on Tarawa during November 1943 wear M3-1XA-1VA1 diaphragm gas masks. The dead Marine is covered by a camouflage poncho. *NA 127-N-70172*

According to PFC 'Josh' Hanafin: 'There were 20 mm anti-aircraft guns on the LCT's [Landing Craft Tracked], twin mounts. The way it was set up, the Marines manned one gun, the Navy the other... Your shoulders would fit into two braces attached to the gun; it gave a hell of a kick!' This weapon was less successful on land as an anti-tank gun, being too heavy to negotiate through jungle swamp or across rugged terrain, being attached to a fixed mount. Some '20 mms' were fixed on mounts belonging to larger calibre towed weapons for mobility. Early in the war some Marine defence battalions used the towed 10-round clip-fed Colt 37 mm M1 anti-aircraft gun, but this was later replaced by the ubiquitous four-round clip-fed Bofors 40 mm M1, and the 3-inch M3. All of these weapons were also employed as anti-tank guns, with varying degrees of success.

Regarding artillery, the Marines used a variety of weapons including the compact 75 mm M1A1 pack howitzer, which initially equipped three of the division's howitzer battalions; and the towed 105 mm M2A1 howitzer, which was issued to one battalion of the division artillery regiment early in the war to provide general fire support. The latter gun had completely replaced the 75mm howitzer by late 1945. The 105 mm M7 self-propelled howitzer unofficially replaced the halftrack-mounted 75 mm M3 gun in May 1945, and was used extensively by the 1st and 6th Marine Divisions at Okinawa.

Fleet Marine Force rocket detachments were armed with 4.5 in. T45 self-propelled rocket launchers, and were later assigned to Marine Divisions as platoons. The T45 consisted of two launcher racks, each containing 14 rockets, which were mounted on an International one ton 4x4 truck. Barrage rocket launchers were mounted aboard infantry landing craft by 1944.

Special weapons battalions used the 37 mm M6 self-propelled anti-tank gun from February 1942

Left from top to bottom; First aid dressing and custom-made pouch; Marine canteens in a well-bleached, early standard cover and in first pattern 'cross flap' cover. The second pattern cover of this type had a small circular hole in the bottom section which permitted it to drain after immersion during river crossings and beach landings. The canteens carried inside these covers were made from various materials. Those surplus from World War One and manufactured at the beginning of the Pacific War were aluminium. Most men carried two canteens suspended from their belts via two wire hooks attached to the back of the canteen cover. *Photos by the author, courtesy of Jim Moran*

Above, pack and '782' gear for a Marine assistant squad leader laid out for inspection at Guadalcanal in 1944. An M1 carbine with magazine pouch and cleaning kit is on the right. His personal grooming kit, including razor, soap dish, tooth brush and powder, sewing kit, mirror and comb, are on the left, below which are placed his 'scivvies', or underwear. His 'meat can', or mess tin, and eating utensils are in the centre, just above which is his canteen cup. In the foreground are his shelter half pins and folding pole with guy line. Next to this is an entrenching tool and canvas cover. Note that a camouflage shelter half has been used as a ground sheet. *NA 127-GW-903-79982*

until mid-1943. Mounted on a 3/4 ton 4x4 truck, forward firing was difficult and necessitated the vehicle being reversed into position before the weapon could be effectively brought into action. The lighter weight 37 mm M3A1 anti-tank gun, copied from the German AT gun, equipped both regimental weapons companies and special weapons battalions in 1942. The 75 mm M3 self-propelled anti-tank gun was issued on the same organisational basis in mid-1944. Known as the Self-Propelled Mount (SPM), it was mainly used by the Marines as an assault weapon for knocking out fortified positions.

As Japanese armour posed only a limited threat in the jungles and swamps of the Pacific Islands, the M1 rocket launcher, or 'bazooka', was initially used on only a small scale by Marine infantry units as an anti-tank weapon. Discovered to be highly effective against bunkers, it saw greater use from mid-1943. During 1944 the slightly modified M1A1 was introduced, but this also began to be replaced by the end of the year by the M9 rocket launcher, which had a greater range due to its longer aluminium tube. The latter feature could be broken down into two sections for transportation. Raider battalions used the larger Boys bolt-action, .55 calibre Mk I anti-tank rifle which was fed by a five-round magazine and fixed to a bipod. Personnel firing bazookas could wear a face mask consisting of M1943 disposable goggles, to which was attached a synthetic coated cotton veil to protect the face from muzzle blast.

Tanks used by the Marines at the beginning of the war included the 17-ton General Stuart M3 and M3A1 light tanks, plus the M3A3 light tank which was introduced in 1942. All three models were mounted with a 37 mm M5 or M6 gun. The M3 tank also carried five .30 calibre M1919A4 and A5 machine guns, while the other models had only three weapons of the same calibre. The M4-series of 33-ton medium tanks came into service in 1944. The General Sherman M4A2

and M4A3 mounted a 75 mm M3 cannon, two M1919A4 and A5 machine guns, and a .50 calibre HB-M2 in the turret. Some M4s were fitted with a flamethrower instead of the 75 mm main gun.

Burrell A. Tipton served in medium tanks within C Company, 6th Regiment, 2nd Marine Division, during the Saipan and Tinian landings in 1944. On Saipan his tank had the distinction of knocking out five tanks of the 9th Japanese Tank Regiment in five minutes! Tipton recalled: 'We got a frantic radio message that the Japanese tanks were on their way. As luck would have it, we were directly in their path. All we had to do was swing the turret around, aim the 75 mm cannon, and three Jap tanks were permanently out of action. An infantryman ran up and told the Lieutenant that two more tanks were just a short ways to our left. We motored over to a small tree covered area, and sure enough, there was two more tanks trying to hide. We quickly added those to our list, and their crews joined their honorable ancestors also.'

Regarding night-time bivouac, Tipton recollected: 'At sundown we usually secured for the night. That meant we would dig a trench the length of the tank, drive over the ditch, and that was our foxhole. The tanks had a trap door in the bottom and after lifting the door out, all we had to do was crawl down through and we were in our fox hole'!

Below left, the Model 1941 haversack arranged as a Light Marching Pack, complete with M1910 entrenching shovel and camouflage poncho, represents the typical combination many Marines carried into combat.

Below right, rear view showing shoulder straps and belt supporting strap at lower centre. *Photos by the author, courtesy of Jim Moran*

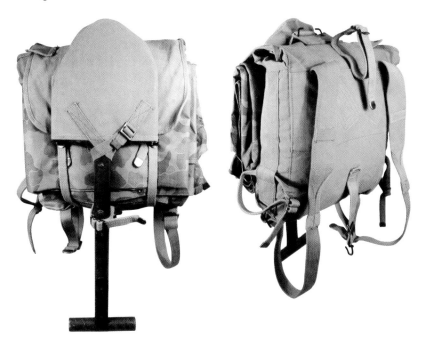

MARINE WAY OF WAR

Opposite, **this group of Marine Raiders, probably from the 3rd Battalion, pose for the camera on Cape Torokina, Bougainville, in November 1943. They all wear first pattern two-piece camouflage utilities. Most have the first pattern M1 helmet covers, although one man still uses camouflage netting. Note the very high pre-war leggings worn by the Marine kneeling at centre. All appear to be armed with M1903A3 Springfield rifles, a weapon much preferred by snipers and other specialist Marine troops.** *US Marine Corps Photo*

Prior to the 20th century, the role of the Marine Corps had always been to provide ships' guards for Navy vessels, to enforce shipboard discipline, to man ships' guns, and to participate in landing parties for very limited operations ashore. Even during the Civil War, Commandant Jacob Zeilin simply did not recognise the amphibious assault mission of the Marine Corps, or else rejected it for being too much like the task of the US Army. Secretary of the Navy Gideon Welles and Assistant Secretary Gustavus V. Fox did not push for the development of such forces, nor was there any interest in doing so in either the War Department or Congress. To assume any other role would be to risk amalgamation with the Army, or absorption into the Navy, which had to be avoided at all cost.

Strangely, it was renewed political antagonism and the continued opposition of some naval officers to its very existence, that encouraged the Marine Corps to develop a more meaningful role at the beginning of the 20th century. During the early part of 1900, the Secretary of the Navy, John D. Long, established the General Board of the Navy to serve as an advisory body to determine future naval policy. Admiral George Dewey was appointed President of the Board while membership consisted of high-ranking officers of the Navy, with the exception of Marine Colonel George C. Reid, who at the time was Adjutant and Inspector of the Marine Corps.

Mindful of the prominent role played by amphibious operations in the defeat of the Spanish in Cuba during 1898, the Board wisely recommended that the 'assault mission', consisting of the seizure of advanced bases and the systematic development of 'advanced base' personnel and equipment, be assigned to the Marine Corps. Meeting with the approval of Secretary of the Navy Long, Marine Commandant George F. Elliott was instructed to carry into effect the plan and shortly thereafter a Marine battalion had been especially organised for the purpose.

By 1902, special training in the capture and defence of advanced bases had begun.

Throughout the remainder of the pre-World War One years, the Marine Corps continued to develop and perfect its advanced base training. In 1910 an advanced base school was established at New London in Connecticut, while unrest in various Latin American countries, such as Nicaragua, Panama, and Mexico, gave the Marines the opportunity to put what they had learned into practice along the way.

The trench warfare in France between 1917-18 gave the Marine Corps a different perspective on warfare, but with the return of peace, new concerns arose regarding the possibility of Japanese domination in the Pacific. To counter this threat, and to strengthen its role in any future war, the Marine Corps continued to develop its strategy and tactics. A staff system was established, within which a Planning Section had responsibility for 'all matters pertaining to plans for operations and training, intelligence, ordnance supplies and equipment'. By 1920, this had been expanded into the Division of Operations and Training under General Logan M. Feland.

One of the officers within this body concerned with war plans was Lieutenant Colonel Earl H. 'Pete' Ellis, whose research and prescient thinking on war in the Pacific contributed much to what ultimately became known as the 'Orange Plan'. Originally entitled 'Operation Plan 712, Advanced Base Operations in Micronesia', the document written by Ellis in 1921 forecast requirements for war in the Pacific, including the size of forces necessary to take a defended beachhead, and the future of amphibious warfare. He prescribed that attacks should take place in daylight to avoid confusion among the landing craft and assault forces. The assault troops should be preceded by a naval version of the World War One 'box barrage', and should be supported throughout the operation by massive aerial attack. The assault force must consist not solely of infantry but also of

Lieutenant Colonel Earl H. 'Pete' Ellis, who in 1921 predicted the form amphibious warfare would take, should a conflict break out between the US and Japan in the Pacific. He died mysteriously on a 'business trip' to the Marshall and Caroline Islands later the same year. *USMC Photo # 127-N-307257*

machine gun units, engineers, artillery, and light tanks in order to penetrate beach defenses. These troops would require special landing craft armed with machine guns and light cannon. Ellis predicted, 'the landing will entirely succeed or fail practically on the beach', and concluded: 'It is not enough that the troops be skilled infantrymen or artillerymen of high morale; they must be skilled watermen and jungle-men who know it can be done—Marines with Marine training.'

Unfortunately, 'Pete' Ellis never lived to see the fruits of his labour. With the collusion of Marine Commandant John A. Lejeune, he took extended leave in May 1921 to visit the Marshall and Caroline Islands. Officially on a 'business trip', he was unofficially conducting a personal reconnaissance of the islands, but died under mysterious circumstances. From henceforth, Ellis was a martyr in the eyes of the Marines and, on 23 July 1921, 'Operation Plan 712' was adopted in its entirety as a guide for Marine Corps war planning, officer training, equipment development, and field exercises.

Ellis had not been alone in realising the future role the Marine Corps would have to play. In February 1922, Commandant Lejeune recommended to the General Board that the primary war mission of the Corps in wartime should be to accompany the Fleet for operations on shore in support of the Fleet. Five years later, the offensive mission for the Marine Corps in amphibious operations was officially defined as being: 'To seize, establish, and defend, until relieved by Army forces, advanced naval bases; and to conduct such limited auxiliary land operations as are essential to the prosecution of the naval campaign.' Subsequent Marine Corps service in the Pacific War from 1942 to 1945 was to extend far beyond this limited concept.

In order to prepare for its future amphibious role, the Marine Corps conducted several landing exercises with the Fleet during the two decades preceding World War Two. The first took place from January to April 1922, when the Advanced Base Force, under command of Lieutenant Colonel Richard M. Cutts, landed at Guantanamo Bay in Cuba, and Culebra in Puerto Rico. On these occasions, artillery gun crews received valuable training, and both light and heavy equipment was tested for use in ship-to-shore operations.

In 1923, the designation 'Advanced Base Force' was dropped and the general term 'Marine Corps Expeditionary Forces' was used in reference to Marine units either permanently or provisionally available for overseas service with the Fleet. Beginning in December 1923, and lasting about three months, Fleet Exercise No. IV saw over 3,300 officers and men of the Marine Corps Expeditionary Force, under Brigadier General Eli K. Cole, land again at Culebra and around the Canal Zone. This action involved the first serious experimentation with landing craft rather than standard ships' boats.

BEETLE BOATS

Two types of landing boats were tested, the first being a derivation of the British 'beetle' boat, used at Suvla Bay during the Gallipoli landings in August 1915. The other boat tested during the winter exercises of 1924 was the 'Christie Tank', an amphibious tank built by the Sun Shipbuilding Company. Kept a secret in order to surprise the defenders of Culebra, the Christie tank, while tested successfully on rivers, proved unseaworthy and was dropped by the Marine Corps, although incredibly the US government sold plans of the test model to the Japanese shortly thereafter.

By 1926, the Beetle boat had been developed into the Motor Troop Lighter, which was a 'special purpose' vessel to be used primarily for the landing of the first troop wave under fire. Propelled by two motors, it was 50-feet long and had a 14-foot beam, and a front hatch for off-loading troops or equipment once it hit the beach. It was armoured against small arms fire, and had the

capacity to carry machine guns or 37 mm guns. Two of these vessels, one loaded with 100 men with heavy marching packs, and the other with a 155 mm gun and its tractor, were successfully trialed later that year.

While various assault vessels were developed, Marine Corps personnel were being educated in the tactical art of amphibious warfare. This was largely the responsibility of the Marine Corps School at Quantico, Virginia, where officers were instructed in the subject of overseas expeditions and ship-to-shore operations from 1925.

Further development of the Corps' greater wartime 'mission' was stalled by Marine involvement in Latin America and China during the latter years of the 1920s. However, efforts were renewed in 1933 when the Secretary of the Navy issued General Order 241 which formally established the Fleet Marine Force, the operational basis for the Marine Corps' future amphibious role in the Pacific. Also created that year was the Marine Corps Equipment Board, also at Quantico. This body continued the testing of *matériel* for landing operations, and defined and developed three different categories of assault vessels—the Landing Boat, used as a carrier of troops from ship-to-shore; the Lighter, for carrying tanks and trucks; and the Amphibian, which was regarded as a fire

support weapon in the 1930s, but evolved into a first wave assault vehicle.

After unsuccessful experimentation with adapted Atlantic fishing craft as landing boats, the Marine Corps Equipment Board became interested in a vessel called the 'Eureka' developed by Andrew Higgins, a New Orleans boat builder. Designed for the use of trappers and oil-drillers along the lower Mississippi River and Gulf Coast, the Eureka had a tunnel stern to protect the propeller and a special type of bow, which Higgins called a 'spoonbill', because it enabled the vessel to run well up on low banks and beaches, and then to retract just as easily. Strangely it was an idea copied from the future enemy, the Japanese, which added the finishing touch to the development of an American landing boat. Tests went on with the Eureka until April 1941, when Major Ernest E. Linsert, Secretary to the Equipment Board, showed Higgins a photograph of a Japanese landing craft with a bow ramp which enabled small vehicles to drive on to the beach, and allowed troops to run ashore. Responding enthusiastically, and with further Navy funding, Higgins quickly evolved the modified US 'Landing Craft, Personnel (Ramp)', and the principle of the amphibious assault had turned full circle.

Adopted for development on a large scale by the Marine Corps, the precursor of the

Marines of the Expeditionary Force wade ashore from a Motor Troop Lighter, or 'Beetle' boat, at Culebra, Puerto Rico, during fleet manoeuvres in 1924. Note the men are emerging from a front hatch in order to jump into the water. *USMC* *Photo # 127-N-515096*

Men of the 1st Battalion, 5th Marines, part of the Fleet Marine Force, wearing fibre tropical helmets as they roll over the side of an old-fashioned ship's launch in a practice landing at Culebra in 1936.
USMC
Photo # 127-N-529463

'Landing Craft, Vehicle, Personnel', or LCVP, used so successfully on the beaches of Guadalcanal and Bougainville, was born. In later years, General Holland Smith would opine that this craft 'did more to win the war in the Pacific than any other single piece of equipment'.

Andrew Higgins was also involved in the final development during May 1942 of a successful Tank Lighter. Capable of carrying the newly developed Army 30-ton medium tank, this 50-foot self-propelled vessel had two parallel hinged ramps in the stern and could be effectively beached stern-to. This was the prototype of the 'Landing Craft, Mechanised', or LCM, which carried so much fire

support ashore in the Pacific.

The predecessor of the amphibian tractor, or Amtrac, was designed in 1935 as a non-military vehicle for the rescue of downed aviators and hurricane victims in the Florida Everglades. The brainchild of Donald Roebling, whose grandfather, Colonel Washington Roebling, had built the famous Brooklyn Bridge, the resulting 'Alligator' was an aluminium-built amphibious vehicle powered by a 92-horsepower Chrysler industrial engine, with a paddle-tread track, similar in principle to early paddle-wheel steamships. Military development of the 'Alligator' began two years later and, by July 1941, the 'Landing Vehicle,

Tracked', or LVT, was set to revolutionise the concept of beach assault in the Pacific.

An adaptation of this vehicle, with a gun turret fitted in place of the cargo compartment, began development during the same period. Designed to serve as an amphibious tank to accompany personnel carriers to the beach, the LVT (Armoured) initially carried a 37 mm gun, while by 1944 the LVT(A)-4 mounted a 75 mm howitzer. The Marine Corps used a total of 18,620 LVTs of various models during the Second World War.

Meanwhile, Marine aviation was mastering the art of close air support for amphibious landings. The air wing of the Corps had practised air support technique in the mountains of Nicaragua during the 1930s, but faster planes made target selection more complex and required more reliable communication between air and ground. By 1938, the ratio of four-to-one numerical superiority in the air was considered essential in order to eliminate the enemy threat in the skies, and to shatter his beachhead defences. Close attention was also paid to the direct assistance aviation could give in guiding landing boats to the beach, laying down smoke screens, and providing reconnaissance and spotting for naval gunfire and artillery.

After the landing, the challenge for Marine aviation was that of applying fire power to destroy specific enemy frontline positions without endangering nearby friendly units. The key to success in this field lay in the establishment of effective communications between the front line troops and the support aircraft. Mistakes at Bougainville and Tarawa, in the Pacific War, were later rectified at Tinian, and came close to perfection at Iwo Jima and Okinawa.

Regardless of these developments, Marine aviation was still in its infancy when World War Two began, with only 251 operational aircraft of all types, and only 2,766 personnel, of whom only about 600 were pilots. The director of Marine aviation was Colonel Ralph J. Mitchell, who had

been awarded the Distinguished Flying Cross for service in Nicaragua. Two Marine Air Wings existed, with Brigadier General Roy S. Geiger commanding the 1st Marine Aircraft Wing at Quantico, and Brigadier General Ross E. Rowell at Hawaii and San Diego with the 2nd Marine Aircraft Wing. By the end of the war, the Marine air arm had grown to 32 aircraft groups and 145 squadrons, flying everything from Vought F4U Corsair fighters to carrier-based B-25, or 'Mitchell', medium bombers, and was manned and maintained by 125,162 personnel. A total of 2,355 Japanese aircraft were destroyed by this force in air combat.

Three 'Alligators', or amphibian tractors, being tested by the Marine detachment at Dunedin, Florida, on 18 September 1941. Invented by Donald Roebling, these craft played a vital role as 'Landing Vehicles, Tracked', or Amtracs, during numerous Pacific island assaults from 1942 to 1945. *USMC Photo # 127-N-529506*

TRIANGULAR REINFORCEMENT

Prior to 1941, the largest Marine formations were the 1st and 2nd Marine Brigades, formed respectively on the East and West coasts of the US in 1935-36. Both of these brigades were constructed around an infantry regiment and an aircraft group. As these units were all under-strength, it was planned to reinforce them with ships' guards if deployed in combat. The 1st and 2nd Marine Divisions were formed in early 1941 by enlarging these two brigades. The 3rd Division was activated during September 1942, while the 4th Division began service in August 1943. Both the 5th and 6th Divisions were organised in 1944.

As the Pacific War developed, so did the composition of the Marine Division. Its nerve centre was the division headquarters battalion, which had headquarters, signal, and military police companies. The infantry regiment remained the core of the division's fighting force. At the beginning of the conflict there were two infantry regiments per division, but soon a third was added, and the 'triangular reinforcement' concept was consolidated, with three battalions per regiment, three companies per battalion, three platoons per company, and three squads per platoon.

The basic organisation of the Marine infantry regiment changed very little during the Pacific War, although its allocation of weapons and manpower did. A headquarters and service company provided command and minimal service support. The regimental weapons company contained three anti-tank and anti-aircraft gun platoons. Each of the three infantry battalions was composed of a headquarters company, three rifle companies and, until 1944, a weapons company. A rifle company contained a large group of headquarters personnel, a weapons platoon, and three rifle platoons.

The weapons platoon consisted of a headquarters contingent, plus mortar and machine gun sections. At the beginning of the war, weaponry consisted of two 60 mm mortars and two .30 calibre M1919A4 machine guns. By April 1943, this had been increased to three of the former and five of the latter. During May 1944, weapons platoons began to be re-designated as machine gun platoons, and were armed with between four and six each of M1919A4 light and M1917A1 heavy machine guns. J. Fred Haley, 1st Battalion, 8th Marines, who served on Tinian during July 1944, recorded: 'Each rifle company had a weapons platoon... When accompanied with Browning automatic rifles and semi-automatic M1 rifles in the rifle platoons, the machine guns formed a tremendous base of firepower.'

Prior to 1944, a rifle platoon was divided into tthree nine-man rifle squads. Each squad had a sergeant as squad leader, an assistant squad leader ranked a corporal, two scouts, three riflemen armed with .03 Springfields or M1 rifles, a grenadier who carried an M1 rifle and grenade launcher, and an automatic rifle man with M1918A2BAR. The automatic rifle squad consisted of a squad leader, armed with an M50 sub-machine gun, two automatic riflemen, and five riflemen. After April 1943, some riflemen were re-designated assistant automatic riflemen, or assistant BAR men, and carried M1 carbines. The platoon headquarters consisted of a 2nd lieutenant platoon leader, a platoon sergeant, plus five radio operators and runners.

An alternative Marine Corps combat squad organisation, essential for the type of combat involved in amphibious assault, had been phased-in by the end of March 1944. Originally adopted and used by Lieutenant Merritt A. Edson, 5th Marines, on jungle patrols during the Nicaraguan Campaign in 1927, it consisted of three- and four-man groups of riflemen focussed around an automatic weapon. By the late 1930s, Major Edson and other 4th Marine officers had further refined these 'fighting teams' while protecting American interests in China. When the 1st and 2nd Raider battalions were organised in 1942, Edson, by then a lieutenant colonel in command of the 1st Battalion, organised the rifle squads on the same basis. The new 4th Marines, formed from the Raider battalions on 1 February 1944, continued to develop the concept. Acknowledged as an effective way for small-unit leaders, trained for independent command in combat, to keep in touch with their men when field communications had broken down under fire, the technique was used to good effect at Eniwetok by the 22nd Marines under Colonel John T. Walker, also during February 1944.

Encouraged by the reports received from these units, Marine Corps headquarters further tested four-man 'fire teams' back in the US using the 24th

Men of the 1st Parachute Battalion prepare for a practice jump at San Diego in 1941. All wear the first-pattern smock over sage green utilities. The man at right has the later pattern canvas-covered hip pocket with external pouch thought to have been added to carry either the Western Cutlery paratrooper knife or immediate-use magazine for the M55 folding stock Reising SMG with which they were armed. Note the chin-straps of their leather jump helmets and elbow pads. Their Marine jump boots are identifiable by the absence of toe caps. They are about to use T4 parachutes.
NA 127-N-402928

1941–1945

Marines, and by the end of March 1944 the rifle company table of organisation had been changed to include them, in place of the automatic rifle squad.

The new rifle squad was composed of a squad leader with the rank of sergeant, who was armed with an M1 carbine. He led three fire teams each consisting of a team leader, with the rank of corporal, and a rifleman, both of whom carried an M1 rifle and M7 grenade launcher; an automatic rifleman armed with a M1918A2 BAR, and an assistant automatic rifleman also armed with a carbine. An infantry battalion was also allocated 27 each of bazookas, flame-throwers, and demolition packs, one of each per rifle squad. The three four-man fire team completed the pattern of triangular organisation down to the smallest possible tactical group.

J. Fred Haley, 1st Battalion, 8th Marines, recalled 'Each regiment on the line held one of its three battalions in reserve; each battalion...held one of its three rifle companies in reserve; and each rifle company... held one of its three rifle platoons in reserve; and each platoon usually held one of its three rifle squads in reserve.'

The divisional artillery regiment went through several reorganisations as it responded to the demands of the Pacific War. This affected both the number of battalions and the calibre of weapons used. Until 1943 there were three 75 mm pack howitzer battalions and one 105 mm battalion per regiment. In April 1943, an additional 105 mm battalion was added, while during May 1944 onwards the 75 mm battalion was converted to 165 mm. Each 75 mm battery had six guns throughout the war, while the 105 mm batteries were increased from four to six pieces.

The engineer regiment was composed of engineer, pioneer, and naval construction battalions (nicknamed CBs or 'SeaBees'), each of which included a headquarters company and three 'line' companies. The former were generally regarded purely as assault engineers, while the SeaBees, who were formed in February 1942, were recruited from among civilian construction workers to perform the more demanding engineering assignments. Becoming detached from engineer regiments by the end of the war, the 238,000 SeaBees were organised into 31 regiments and 388 battalions, plus numerous other smaller units.

At the beginning of the war, a divisional light tank battalion consisted of four tank companies which operated 18 M3-series tanks, divided into three platoons of five, and one headquarters platoon of three tanks. During April 1943, each battalion lost one company, which went into the newly forming

Marine divisions. In May 1944, each battalion was authorised M4-series tanks, and 'light' was dropped from their unit designation. Each company was entitled to 15 tanks, with four per platoon and three in headquarters. Often units continued to operate with a mixture of M3 and M4 vehicles.

RAIDERS AND PARATROOPERS

The Raider battalions provided the Marine Corps with light, mobile forces at the beginning of the Pacific conflict. The organisation of these units was stimulated by the visit of two Marine officers, Captain (later General) Samuel B. Griffith II and Captain (later Marine Commandant) Wallace M. Greene, plus 20 enlisted men, to Scotland where they trained with the British Commandos between November 1941 and February 1942. Upon their return to the US, the 1st Separate Battalion, later re-designated the 1st Raider Battalion, was formed under Lieutenant Colonel Merritt 'Red Mike' Edson at Quantico, from the 1st Battalion, 5th Marines. Initially attached to the 1st Marine Division, this unit was transferred to Amphibious Forces, Atlantic Fleet. The 2nd Raider Battalion, under Lieutenant Colonel Evans F. Carlson, was organised on 4 February, while the 3rd and 4th Battalions were set up between September and December 1942. The last of these units was shipped out to the Pacific by February 1943.

The special purpose of these Raider units was to spearhead amphibious landings on beaches generally thought to be inaccessible; conduct raiding expeditions requiring surprise and speed; and engage in guerrilla type operations for lengthy periods of time behind enemy lines.

The 1st and 2nd Raider Battalions participated in some of the heaviest fighting during the early stages of the Pacific War. Edson's Raiders swooped on Tulagi Island prior to the Guadalcanal landings on 7 August 1942. Ten days later, two companies of Carlson's Raiders conducted the Makin Island Raid, during which they went ashore from two large submarines and, in true commando-style, took on the Japanese garrison, shot up two seaplanes landing reinforcements, blew up the radio station, and burned supplies, before finally being taken off again by the subs. Nine Marines were left behind during the confusion surrounding the withdrawal, and were beheaded by the Japanese who re-took the island.

Meanwhile, Edson's Raiders had moved from Tulagi to Guadalcanal, where they distinguished themselves during the landing at Taivu Point and defence of Henderson Field in September 1942. Also on Guadalcanal by the following month, Carlson's Raiders embarked on a classic jungle patrol, marching 150 miles during which they fought a dozen actions, killed 500 enemy, and successfully drove the remainder into the inhospitable interior.

The 2nd and 3rd Raider battalions, under Lieutenant Colonels Joseph S. McCaffery and Fred S. Beans, suffered heavy casualties during their more than two months ashore on Bougainville during November/December 1943 as they fought beside Army and Marine Corps troops. From the outset, many had opposed the creation of specialised Raider battalions, believing that all Marine units were capable of raider-style operations by the very nature of their training. During January 1944, the Raiders were finally reorganised as conventional infantry. The 4th Marines, lost when Corregidor was overrun in 1942, was reformed almost entirely from their ranks on 1 February 1944. The 1st, 3rd and 4th Raider battalions became the 1st, 2nd, and 3rd battalions of 4th Marines, while the 2nd Battalion became Weapons Company of the same unit.

The Marine Parachute troops, known unofficially during the Second World War as 'Marine Paratroopers', began formation on 28 May 1941 with training of the first parachutists at Lakehurst, New Jersey, during the following October. Parachute schools were opened at San Diego, California, and New River, South Carolina, during February and May of 1942 respectively. By March 1942, A Company, 1st Parachute Battalion, had completed its organisation. The four battalions of Parachute troops eventually formed were re-organised during April 1943 into the 1st Parachute Regiment. Only the first three battalions were operational when these units were finally disbanded in January/February 1944.

Ironically, the only combat jump performed by Marine Paratroopers was in southern France as part of an OSS unit. Two unit combat jumps were planned in the Pacific, at Kolombangara and Kavieng, but were subsequently cancelled. However, paratroopers did perform valuable service as infantry. They first saw action at Tulagi and Guadalcanal, where the 1st Battalion, under Major Robert H. Williams, landed at the harbour inlet of Gavutu and, after overcoming bitter Japanese opposition and receiving 20 per cent casualties, planted the 'Stars and Stripes' on the top of Hill 148. Moved to Guadalcanal at the end of September 1942, they were grouped with Edson's Raiders and fought at 'Bloody Ridge', where they sustained a further 128 casualties. Due to the demand for increased Marine manpower, the 1st Parachute Regiment was disbanded on 29 February 1944, and members were transferred

to form the 28th Marines, which became the nucleus of the 5th Marine Division. Some former Paratroopers also served with the 6th Marine Division and III Amphibious Corps.

COMBAT GROUPS AND LANDING TEAMS

By 1942, the Fleet Marine Force contained a pool of combat support and service units for special duties, and for attachment to amphibious corps or divisions during an assault landing. These included a war dog platoon, a provisional rocket detachment, a signal intelligence platoon, an amphibian truck company, plus various artillery, and amphibian tractor, or Amtrac, battalions. Marine regiments reinforced by these units were initially called 'combat groups', and their attached units were known as 'combat teams'. Towards the end of 1943, these designations were changed to 'regimental landing teams' and 'battalion landing teams' respectively.

In conjunction with the assault on Guadalcanal in August 1942, the 1st Marine Division formed Combat Group A, based on the 5th Marines, while Combat Group B was organised around the 1st Marines. Both Groups were divided into three Combat Teams, each of which consisted of an infantry battalion, a 75 mm pack howitzer battery, plus engineer, pioneer, and amphibian tractor platoons. Further combat support and service units, including the 1st Parachute Battalion, formed an additional support group for the Marine Division.

Regimental and battalion landing teams were first adopted for the attack on Betio Island, in Tarawa Atoll, during November 1943. The first assault wave consisted of Regimental Landing Teams 2 and 8, the designation of which was based on that of their parent regiments, the 2nd and 8th Marines. Besides infantry battalions, both of these RLTs included a 105 mm artillery battalion, an Amtrac battalion, plus other combat support and service units.

Battalion landing teams within each RLT were called 'Red', 'White', and 'Blue', and were based around the 1st, 2nd, and 3rd Battalions respectively. These units were supplemented by a 75 mm pack howitzer battalion, a tank company, and an engineer platoon.

By early 1944, Marine battalions and companies of the 4th Marine Division were being organised into 'assault and demolition teams' for the landings on Roi-Namur, in the Marshall Islands. Infantry companies were formed into six teams, each of which manned an Amtrac. Each team was led by an officer and consisted of a four-man light machine gun section, a five-man demolition group carrying dynamite packs, a three-man bazooka team, and a four-man support party armed with two Browning automatic rifles. Reserve companies following-up in Higgins boats, or LCVPs, formed 'boat teams' based on the same structure, minus the machine gun section.

Later that year, every battalion in both the 4th and 5th Divisions had formed a provisional 'assault platoon', armed with 'blowtorches, bazookas, pineapples, and corkscrews', or flame-throwers, rocket launchers, grenades, and demolition packs. On Iwo Jima, these divisions restructured their rifle platoons to include two rifle squads and a 'demolition squad'. The latter had a 'pin-up team', armed with two BARs and a bazooka, whose job it was to pin the enemy down; a 'demolition team' carrying satchel charges and bangalore torpedoes, to destroy the enemy; and a 'flame-thrower team' escorted by riflemen, to make sure the enemy was dead!

One of the most tragic mishaps of the Pacific War occurred during the Roi-Namur operation. While mopping up a large concrete blockhouse, an assault team of the 2nd Battalion, 24th Marines, hurled a satchel charge inside the gun port, and seconds later a huge explosion rocked the whole island. The blockhouse had been crammed with torpedo warheads, which blew a mushroom cloud thousands of feet in the air, killing and wounding at least 57 Marines, and raining down huge concrete chunks all around. Watching from an aircraft above the beaches, Major C. F. Duchein, a 4th Division air observer, remarked, 'Great God Almighty! The whole damn island's blown up!'

NAVAJO CODE TALKERS

The Navajo 'code talkers' took part in every assault the US Marines conducted in the Pacific from 1942 to 1945. They served in all six Marine divisions, Raider battalions and parachute units, transmitting messages by telephone and radio in their native language—a code that the Japanese never broke. The idea to use Navajo for secure communications came from Philip Johnston, the son of a missionary to the Navajos and one of the few non-Navajos who spoke their language fluently. Raised on the Navajo reservation, Johnston was a First World War veteran who knew of the military's search for a code that would withstand all attempts to decipher it. He believed Navajo answered that requirement because it is an unwritten language of extreme complexity.

Early in 1942, Johnston met with Major General Clayton B. Vogel, the commanding general of Amphibious Corps, Pacific Fleet, and his staff, to convince them of the value of the Navajo language

Navajo code talkers PFC Peter Nahaidinae, PFC Joseph Gatewood, and Corporal Lloyd Oliver, 1st Marine Division, in the Southwest Pacific during 1944. The Marine Corps enlisted over 200 Navajos to serve as radiomen. Speaking in their native tongue, US radio communications proved too difficult for the Japanese to decipher. *US Marine Corps Photo*

as a code. He staged tests under simulated combat conditions, demonstrating that Navajos could encode, transmit and decode a three-line message in English in 20 seconds. Machines of the time required 30 minutes to perform the same job!

Impressed by what he saw, Vogel recommended that the Marine Corps enlist 200 Navajos. In May 1942, the first 29 Navajo recruits attended boot camp. Shortly after this, they created the Navajo code at Camp Pendleton, Oceanside, California. This involved the development of a dictionary and numerous words for military terms, all of which had to be memorised during training.

Once a Navajo code talker had completed his training, he was sent to a Marine unit deployed in the Pacific theatre. The code talkers primary duty was to transmit information on tactics and troop movements, orders and other vital battlefield communications, via telephone and radio. They also acted as runners and performed general Marine duties. During the battle for Iwo Jima, Major Howard Connor, a 5th Marine Division signal officer, had six Navajo code talkers working around the clock. During the first two days of the battle, they sent and received over 800 messages, all without error. At the end of the war, Connor declared, 'Were it not for the Navajos, the Marines would never have taken Iwo Jima.'

MARINES
IN COMBAT

To be a Marine and not a rifleman was unthinkable. Despite all the innovation and technology, the heart of Marine Corps training throughout the Pacific War continued to evolve around marksmanship. This was summarised in 'The Riflemen's Creed', written by a general in the Second World War, and which every Marine recruit to this day has to learn by heart: 'This is my rifle. There are many like it, but this one is mine. My rifle is my best friend... Without my rifle, I am useless. I must fire my rifle true. I must shoot straighter than my enemy who is trying to kill me. I must shoot him before he shoots me... Before God I swear this creed. My rifle and I are the defenders of my country. We are the saviours of my life. So be it, until there is no enemy, but Peace!'

Nearly 45,000 men joined the Marine Corps during the first three months after Pearl Harbor. Having hired the advertising firm, J. Walter Thompson Inc., to organise recruiting, weekly enlistment soon soared from 552 to nearly 6,000 men per week. Recruiting posters offered 'Japanese hunting licences', and appealed to the nation's toughest, most physically fit, young patriots to wear the 'Globe and Anchor'.

The hard-pressed recruiting depots of 1942 began to concentrate on creating Marines, rather than just infantrymen, out of the eager hordes who rushed to enlist. Driven remorselessly by veteran drill instructors, the recruits, or 'boots', drilled, marched, hiked, exercised, and learned the rudiments of Marine Corps custom and tradition. They also learned a new vocabulary which turned toilets into 'heads', floors into 'decks', a kitchen into a 'galley', a door into a 'hatch', and a rifle into a 'piece'.

Sergeant William Manchester, 29th Marines, whose memoirs were later published in *Goodbye, Darkness*, recollected his days in 'boot camp': '...the Corps begins its job of building men by destroying the identity they brought with them. Their heads are shaved. They are assigned numbers. The DI [Drill Instructor] is their god.

He treats them with utter contempt. I am told that corporal punishment has since been banned... but in my day it was quite common to see a DI bloody a man's nose, and some boots were gravely injured, though I know of none who actually died.'

Samuel B. Griffith, II, who commanded the 1st Marine Raiders at Guadalcanal, recalled: 'They were a motley bunch. Hundreds were young recruits only recently out of boot training at Parris Island. Others were older; first sergeants yanked off "planks" in Navy yards, sergeants from recruiting duty, gunnery sergeants who had fought in France, perennial privates with disciplinary records a yard long. These were the professionals, the "Old Breed" of United States Marines. Many had fought "Cacos" in Haiti, "bandidos" in Nicaragua, and French, English, Italian, and American soldiers and sailors in every bar in Shanghai, Manila, Tsingtao, Tientsin, and Peking.

'They were inveterate gamblers and accomplished scroungers, who drank hair tonic in preference to post exchange beer... cursed with wonderful fluency, and never went to chapel... unless forced to. Many dipped snuff, smoked rank cigars or chewed tobacco... They could live on jerked goat, the strong black coffee they called "boiler compound," and hash cooked in a tin hat.

'Many wore expert badges with bars for proficiency in rifle, pistol, machine gun, hand grenade, auto-rifle, mortar and bayonet. They knew their weapons and they knew their tactics. They knew they were tough and they knew they were good. There were enough of them to leaven the Division and to impart to the thousands of younger men a share both of the unique spirit which animated them and the skills they possessed.'

Later in the war, Captain George P. Hunt, who lost two-thirds of his men capturing part of the Umurbrogol ridge on Peleliu in 1944, gave the following description of his command: 'Among the 235 of Company K were every type, tall and short, stocky and thin, fair and dark, but unifying them into

one driving spirit was an unshakeable loyalty to each other, a unity far deeper than mere comradeship, and governed by a stern, silent code of mutual respect which could not be broken by a man in battle without his incurring the humiliating contempt of former friends. This was a force that would never allow them to let each other down and that would impel them to perform acts of bravery which, in the normal circumstances of peace, would seem incredible.'

GUADALCANAL

The advanced echelons of Marine Corps recruits who responded to the call in 1942 were shipped out to bases in the Pacific such as Samoa, New Caledonia, or Wellington, New Zealand, where they underwent further training and acclimatisation before finally becoming 'battle ready'. PFC Thomas M. Hanafin, 6th Marines, recalled of his outward voyage: 'It was brutally hot inside the ship which made sleeping very difficult. We spent most of the days on deck where there was a nice, cool breeze. At night we were allowed to sleep on the deck if you could find a spot to spread your body. We'd bring our white sheets and sack out. It was beautiful just laying there, looking up at the sky. It was so peaceful! The sky seemed filled with millions of stars.'

Map showing the location of the main amphibious landings conducted by the Marine Corps during the Pacific War.

Reality set in once the Marines had reached their advanced training camps. According to J. Paul Dupree, 1st Battalion, 10th Marines, they soon 'became inured to the conditions of Samoa, its heat, its almost constant rainfall (196 inches per year was the official average), the mud, the mold, dampness and rusting of everything metal, and mail call came at about six week intervals.'

Eight months to the day after Pearl Harbor, the Marines took the offensive at Guadalcanal, a humid, jungle-covered island in a remote group known as the Solomon Islands, which lie on the north-eastern approaches to Australia. If occupied by the Japanese, they could be used to cut the sea supply route between America and Australia. In US hands they could firstly serve as a shield for the Allied build-up in Australia, and secondly as a springboard for an offensive against the Japanese in the South Pacific.

The action about to take place on 7 August 1942 represented the first US amphibious landings in time of war since 1898. On paper, 'Operation Watchtower' looked good. The 1st Marine Division, fondly known as 'The Old Breed', reinforced by Marine Raider and parachute units, was to land and establish a 'permanent lodgement' on Guadalcanal Island and nearby Tulagi Island. In practice it proved a little less viable. Not fully up to war strength, the

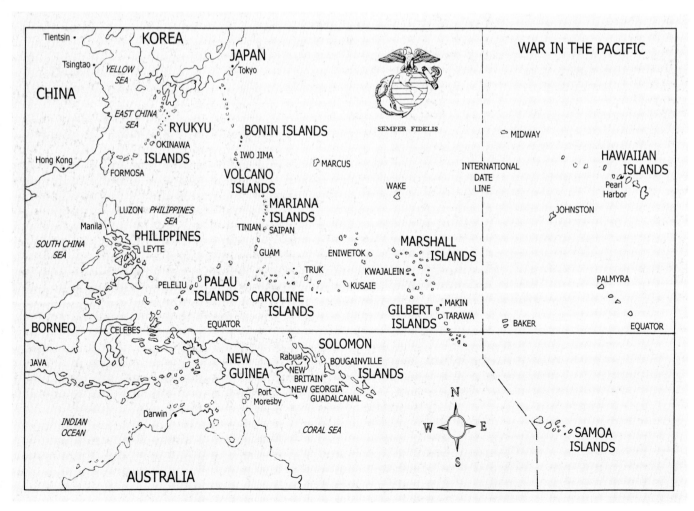

1st Division depended on a hard core of seasoned Marines who knew their weapons and tactics, but who were supplemented by new recruits with little experience beyond elementary drill and weapons training. Furthermore, the division had not taken part in any large-scale exercises, while many of its units had no experience of amphibious landings. Before his departure for the Pacific, commander Major General Alexander A. Vandergrift had been advised that his division would probably not see combat until some time in 1943. When he arrived in New Zealand on 25 June, he received instructions from Vice Admiral Robert L. Ghormley, commander of the South Pacific area, that he had five weeks to prepare for the invasion of Guadalcanal!

Given time, the 1st Division could have been trained and prepared thoroughly for the operation. But the urgency of preventing the Japanese from consolidating their landings on Guadalcanal, begun by the middle of June, dictated otherwise. Washington reluctantly agreed to two postponements of D-Day—first to 4 August and then to 7 August, but made it perfectly clear that the latter date was final. Vandergrift conducted hastily prepared rehearsals for the operation off Koro in the Fijis on 26 July. As coral prevented many units from landing on the beaches, boats broke down with mechanical failure, and aerial

dive-bombing and ships' gunfire proved wildly inaccurate, one observer commented that the whole exercise was 'a fiasco, a complete bust!' Vandergrift consoled himself with the thought that a poor full dress rehearsal presaged a good final performance 'on the night'.

At dawn on 7 August 1942, Australian coast-watcher Martin Clemens, who had first reported the Japanese landings on Guadalcanal, observed what he called 'a fleet majestical' as the grey US transport ships and large infantry landing craft, or LCI(L)s, deployed to their allocated positions off the island coast, while a fleet of five cruisers and nine destroyers loomed ominously behind, salvoes from their guns reverberating around the jungle-covered hillsides.

At 0641 hours, thousands of tense Marines of 'Transport Group X-Ray', organised in 36-man 'boat teams', received the order to scramble down the cargo nets suspended from the decks of the transports. The sea was calm as they pulled away to form into 'boat groups', which then moved towards the beach in regular waves. As the boats of the first assault wave, Combat Group A, consisting of the 1st and 3rd Battalions, 5th Marines, under ex-World War One veteran Colonel LeRoy P. Hunt, shuddered to a halt on the white sands, the ships' gunfire and aerial bombardment was lifted to targets further

Heavily-laden riflemen of the 3rd Marine Division clamber down netting from a transport vessel into a Higgins boat, to be transported to the beachhead at Empress Augusta Bay during the assault on Bougainville Island, which began on 1 November 1943. A war dog, possibly belonging to the 1st Marine War Dog Platoon, goes over the side in a sling. Breeds such as German Shepherds and Dobermans were used extensively by the Marines to sniff out snipers and to carry messages.
Imperial War Museum, Photo # NYF 11373

inland. So far, all went according to plan. The boat ramps splashed into the warm, greenish-blue water, and the Marines waded ashore on 'Red Beach' with their weapons held high. This was the moment every man dreaded. Expecting to be met with a wall of withering enemy gunfire, they were amazed and relieved to find that none came. The 2,200 Japanese on the island had been completely surprised by the sudden attack and abandoned their positions, retreating inland.

At this point things began to go wrong as Marine Combat Group B, the second assault wave composed of the 1st Marines, passed through Hunt's men who were digging-in on the beach. Due to faulty intelligence, Colonel Clifton B. Cates, another World War One veteran, found that his main objective, 'Grassy Knoll' or Mount Austen, an eminence which dominated the region from the south, lay about four rather than two miles distant, and through dense jungle. Furthermore, as the day wore on and men and supplies continued to pour onto 'Red Beach', the situation degenerated into chaos as artillery, tanks, jeeps, and trucks rolled ashore; ammunition and fuel was piled up unceremoniously; and Marines arriving in later assault waves wandered around on the sands, waiting for someone to tell them what to do.

If they had met with serious opposition at this stage, the Marines may well have come to grief. Lessons clearly had to be learned, and they were, in the scores of subsequent amphibious operations of the Pacific War. But for the time being, the 1st Marine Division focussed its attention on work still to be done at Guadalcanal.

NO AIR STIRS HERE

As Cates' command moved off the beaches, many had their first real experience of the jungle. The general impression was one of foul decay. 'No air stirs here', one man remembered, 'and the hot humidity is beyond the imagining of anyone who has not lived in it. Rot lies everywhere just under the texotic lushness. The ground is porous with decaying vegetation, emitting a sour, unpleasant odour... Dampness, thick and heavy, is everywhere... [The rain is] unbelievably torrential in season, never ceasing altogether for more than a few days at a time.'

The 5th Marines advanced slowly west along the coast towards Kukum. Pushing inland through the jungle towards 'Grassy Knoll', the 1st Marines quickly became exhausted. Lieutenant Colonel Griffith recollected, 'The men, who had been cooped up in the steaming holds of overcrowded transports for two weeks, were in a deplorable condition. Burdened with excessively heavy packs and extra ammunition, blasted by the heat and stupefying humidity, short of water and salt tablets, they were in no condition to press forward, much less to fight.'

Earlier that day the 1st Raiders of 'Transport Group Yoke' had approached 'Blue Beach' on the western end of Tulagi. They, too, had suffered from lack of exercise and crowded quarters, but unlike the 5th and 1st Marines, were stripped down to minimum equipment for combat. The Raider commander, Lieutenant Colonel Merritt Edson, expected a fierce fight and advised his men, 'Don't worry about food. There's plenty there. Japs eat too. All you have to do is get it.' Although they

Opposite, Marines in the Solomon Islands jungle in 1942. Note the combat cameraman in the foreground. *Peter Newark's Military Pictures*

Above, this painting by Marine Corps war artist Harry Reeks depicts a machine gun post at Henderson Field on Guadalcanal. *Anne S. K. Brown Military Collection*

Next page, men from the 2nd Marine Raider Battalion return from a night patrol on Bougainville. All wear the first-pattern camouflage utilities and helmet covers. Note the 'dog-tags' around the patrol leader's neck. Dog-tags issued to Navy and Marine Corps personnel were circular in shape, as opposed to Army ones which were rectangular. *Imperial War Museum Photo # NYF 10929*

too landed unopposed, their Higgins boats grounded on the coral reef which ringed that part of the coast, and the Raiders were required to wade ashore. Samuel Griffith recalled, 'As the men struggled in waist-deep water to find footing on the slime-coated coral, many carrying heavy loads— mortar tubes, base plates and radio packs—went under. Yanked to their feet, they were propelled shoreward. Those who fell rose with hands bloodied by coral outcroppings, dungaree trousers ripped, and knees gory. Still, by 8:15, assault companies were ashore and the executive officer signalled Edson "Landing successful, no opposition."'

Back on Guadalcanal, Colonel Cates received orders about midnight to forget the 'Grassy Knoll' and swing west towards the Lunga River to capture the nearby airstrip, which was found abandoned by the following afternoon, and christened 'Henderson Field'. Then the Japanese struck from the air, as 40 bombers from the Japanese 8th Fleet, commanded by Vice Admiral Mikawa, attacked the American transports off Guadalcanal, shooting down 93 fighters operating from three US carriers manoeuvring 100 miles south of the Solomons. Pleading a shortage of fuel, the Navy carriers steamed further south. Losing three cruisers, the Battle of Savo, or 'Iron Bottom Sound', was a very costly affair for the US Navy. Before the end of that

day, another Japanese task force sank more transports off 'Red Beach', and by the following morning the remaining US ships had slipped away. The 1st Marine Division was on its own. There were 11,125 Marines on Guadalcanal, and 6,805 on the neighbouring islands. Stranded, short of food and ammunition, their long ordeal now began.

On 21/22 August, the 1st Marines had their first crucial contest as the Japanese counter-attacked on the ground. The main assault came in the form of a series of banzai charges against the American north-east flank across 'Alligator Creek', at Henderson Field. Forewarned, the defenders decimated the Japanese with machine gun fire. Sending his reserve battalion supported by a platoon of light tanks, around behind Colonel Kiyanao Ichiki's forces, Vandergrift forced the Japanese into the sea, following which Ichiki burned his colours and committed *hara-kiri*.

On 8 September, the 1st Raider Battalion and 1st Parachute Battalion made an amphibious landed at Taivu Point, along the northwest coast of Guadalcanal Island, capturing stores and equipment, and gaining intelligence about an impending Japanese attack. Five days later, this attack was driven off during the 'battle of Bloody Ridge' with 1,200 Japanese left dead.

Reinforcements were received on the island by both sides during the remainder of September and beginning of October 1942, as the Japanese II Division, amounting to 80,000 troops, and headquarters of the XVII Army, was transferred to Tenaro, and US forces, including the 7th Marines and the 164th Infantry Regiment, arrived at Henderson Field.

Two further major Japanese assaults were launched on the south end of the air strip on 23/24 October. During driving rain, the defenders hung on tenaciously to their positions, and Sergeant John Basilone, 1st Battalion, 7th Marines, became one of the first enlisted Marines to win the Medal of Honor in World War Two. During the fiercest of fire-fights,

Painting by Harry Reeks of battle on Guadalcanal.
Anne S. K. Brown Military Collection

he repeatedly repaired guns and ducked back through the jungle to the company command post for more ammo belts and spare parts. After one such trip, he returned to find that the enemy had overrun the section of machine guns on his right. Accompanied by one private, he raced to the pit, found eight Japanese, and killed them all. Turning the two guns back on the Japs, he rolled from gun to gun feeding new crews with bullet belts. After the action, over 800 Japanese were found dead in front of Basilone's position!

On short rations, and soaked by tropical rains in the jungle heat, one third of the men under Vandergrift's command contracted malaria. The *Time* correspondent Robert Sherrod later reported: 'Living conditions were appalling... When a man could get away for a bath in the Lunga River, the only time he could take his clothes off, he frequently found there wasn't any soap. If he didn't catch malaria from the Anopheles mosquitoes which swarmed into his foxhole, he was almost certain to get dysentery that tormented his bowels...'

William Manchester remembered of Guadalcanal: '...the typical Marine... ran a fever, wore stinking dungarees, loathed twilight, and wondered whether the US Navy still existed. He ate mouldy rations and quinine. He alternatively shivered and sweated. If he was bivouacked near Henderson, he spent his morning filling in craters left by enemy bombers the night before. If he was on his way back to the line, he struggled through shattered, stunted cocoa-nut trees, scraggy bushes, and putrescent jungle, clawing up and down slopes ankle-deep in mud, hoping he could catch a few hours of uninterrupted sleep in his foxhole. Usually he was disappointed.'

Despite appalling conditions, a Marine was not permitted off the firing line until his temperature had reached 103 degrees. But somehow they managed to hold on at Guadalcanal, turning back repeated large-scale Japanese attacks. Finally, between 1-15 December 1942, the 1st Marine Division was relieved by the 14th Army Corps. The six-month battle for Guadalcanal cost the Marine Corps more than 3,000 casualties, excluding 8,580 cases of malaria. The Japanese lost 25,000 men, 600 planes, and 24 warships. The US Navy also lost 24 warships. But the Japanese advance across the Pacific had been stopped in its tracks, and was never again resumed.

ON TO BOUGAINVILLE

The US Joint Chiefs of Staff next developed two possible plans to defeat Japan. General Douglas MacArthur suggested a push north to New Guinea. This would facilitate the recapture of the Philippines, which could then be used as a base

In this painting, Harry Reeks captures the mood and tension of the jungle patrol on Bougainville during 1943. *Anne S. K. Brown Military Collection*

from which to finally invade Japan. Meanwhile Admirals Nimitz and Halsey proposed an alternative plan which involved using the islands of the central Pacific as stepping stones to Japan. In the true spirit of compromise, both plans were adopted.

Before these two forces could go their separate ways, the large Japanese base at Rabaul, on New Britain Island, had to be eliminated. To this end a Marine Raider battalion seized the Russell Islands northwest of Guadalcanal, in February 1943. Five months later, the US Army made a series of successful landings on New Georgia. The next step—Bougainville, would be a much greater challenge for the Marine Corps.

The largest of the Solomon Islands, Bougainville was defended by an estimated 25,000 Japanese. Once captured it could be used as the site for an airfield that would bring the Allies within land-based fighter range of Rabaul. The 3rd Marine Division, under Major General Allen H. Turnage, a veteran of France, Haiti, and China, landed at Cape Torokina on 1 November 1943, with the 37th Infantry Division in reserve. Turnage's command was divided into two assault teams – the 3rd Marines plus the 2nd Raider Battalion, and the 9th Marines plus the 3rd Raider Battalion. Landing on 12 beaches from Torokina northward, the Marines received little help from four fire-support destroyers which sent salvo after salvo into the water offshore as the landing craft battled ashore. Thankfully the six Marine air squadrons supporting the operation were more successful, giving good covering fire.

The 9th Marines had 86 landing craft wrecked by the rough surf, while on the extreme right, the 1st Battalion, 3rd Marines, met the strongest resistance from a lone Japanese infantry company which manned 18 pillboxes and one casemented 75 mm gun. The latter sank four landing craft and damaged ten others before the Marines reached the beach. PFC Peter Bowman described the procedure for struggling through the surf from boat to beach during actions like that off Bougainville: 'Men on the right hand side of the landing craft disembark over the front corner of the ramp and step off to the right oblique, while those on the opposite side move similarly to the left. The coxswain keeps the engines turning in order to prevent the boat turning sideways... Draw in your breath. Hold your piece at high port. Keeping moving. Churn through the foam. Don't try to run or the drag of the waves will upset your balance. Proceed diagonally through the swirling surf with feet wide apart.'

One of the first men ashore on Cape Torokina was Sergeant Robert A. Owens, of Greenville, South Carolina, who almost single-handedly silenced the 75 mm gun. Seeing his comrades fall to its fire, Owens charged the casemate, dived in through the fire-port, and drove the crew out through the rear exit, before he fell dead of multiple wounds. Posthumously awarded the Medal of Honor, the citation recognised his brave action as 'indomitable and aggressive in the face of certain death'.

The 14,000 Marines who managed to survive the fire-fight on the beach, knocked out the remaining pillboxes, and spent a rain-filled night huddled three to a foxhole, with one man awake and on the look-out for Jap infiltrators.

Once ashore, the main task for the Marines was to build an airstrip and expand and consolidate the perimeter. Until finally relieved in late December by two Army Divisions, the Marines pushed north and east until they had secured a series of hills west of the Torokina River. The appalling conditions encountered in the rain-filled jungle were summed up by a veteran artillery officer of the 12th Marines: '...the oppressive heat, the continuous rain, the knee-deep mud, the dark overgrown tangled forest with the nauseous smell of the black earth and rotting vegetation, all combined to make this one of the most physically miserable operations that our troops were engaged in during the war.' A corporal quipped: '...what we ought to do when the war is over is to give Bougainville to the Japs—and make 'em live on the damned place forever!' One month later, and after a series of battles including Koromakina Lagoon, and 'Hellzapoppin Ridge', Bougainville had fallen at a cost to the 3rd Marine Division of 423 killed and 1,418 wounded.

By the end of 1943, 1st Marine Division, now commanded by General William H. Rupertus, had been replenished and re-equipped in Australia. The day after Christmas, it stormed ashore at Cape Gloucester on the western tip of New Britain, in the last phase of the campaign to capture Rabaul. The initial landings of 'Operation Dexterity' were practically unopposed, although one man was killed by a falling tree, while landing craft coxswains were blinded and confused by an aerial smoke screen laid down by the Fifth Air Force. Stiff resistance was encountered further inland from the 75,000 Japanese defenders. Labelled 'Damp Flat' on the maps, the approaches to the Japanese-held airdrome consisted of jungle swamp forest, described by one Marine as 'damp up to your neck'!

SUICIDE CREEK

After capturing Cape Gloucester airfield, the Marines were ordered to take a Japanese strong-point about a mile east at Borgen Bay called Hill 660. Pushing their way through un-penetrated

Jungle fighting on
Bougainville in 1943
painted by Harry Reeks.
*Anne S. K. Brown
Military Collection*

jungle and endless rain, it took two weeks and three hard fights before the men of the 7th Marines and 3rd Battalion, 5th Marines, achieved their objective. The most ferocious Japanese stand took place along a narrow stream with steep banks which the Marines dubbed 'Suicide Creek'.

Interviewing men who survived the action, Sergeant A. C. Bordages, a Marine combat correspondent, recorded: 'The Marines didn't know the creek was a moat before an enemy strongpoint ...Only snipers shot at the Marine scouts who crossed the creek, feeling their way through the thickets. More Marines followed... The jungle exploded in their faces. They hit the deck, trying to deploy in the bullet-lashed brush and strike back. Marines died there, firing blindly, cursing because they couldn't see the men who were killing them... All day... Marine detachments felt for a gap or soft spot in the enemy's positions... They'd be blasted by invisible machine guns and leave a few more Marines dead in the brush as they fell back across the creek. Then they'd do it all over again.

'There was nothing else they could do. There is no other way to fight a jungle battle — not in such terrain, when the enemy is dug in and your orders are to advance. You don't know where the enemy is. His pillboxes are so camouflaged that you can usually find them only when they fire on you. So you push out scouts... then patrols from different directions until they too draw fire. Thus you locate the enemy. Then you have to take the emplacements, the pillboxes, one by one in desperate little battles.'

After two days of stalemate, Suicide Creek was taken when the 17th Marines, divisional engineers under Colonel H. E. Rosecrans, bulldozed a causeway which permitted the new Sherman tanks, a welcome addition to the Marine Corps, to rumble their way across.

At their next obstacle, an area of high ground called Aogiri Ridge, three assault battalions ground to a halt in the face of intense fire from 37 Japanese bunkers linked by underground tunnels. Fearful he might lose the tenuous grip his men had managed to establish on the ridge, Lieutenant Colonel Lewis W. Walt, leading the 3rd Battalion, 5th Marines, called up the unit's one available 37 mm M3A1 anti-tank gun, loaded with canister and, while appealing for volunteers, he and his runner put their shoulders against the gun wheels and attempted to push the weapon up the ridge in the thick of enemy gunfire. According to Colonel John T. Selden, commanding the 5th Marines: 'Immediately on seeing their new battalion commander and his orderly on the gun, Walt had plenty of volunteers.' Stopping every few

yards to re-load the gun, more Marines replaced those who fell dead or wounded. Reaching the top of the ridge, Walt's men clung to the forward slope only about ten yards from the remaining Japanese positions. After beating off five Jap bayonet charges during the following night, the fight was over and the prize was renamed 'Walt's Ridge'.

After two further days of probing, much of it crawling uphill through mud and jungle slime, the 3rd Battalion, 7th Marines, under Lieutenant Colonel Henry W. Buse, finally captured Hill 660 in a desperate rush on the evening of 14 January 1944. Two combat correspondents who went through hell from 'Suicide Creek' to Hill 660 reported: 'The boys were tired, wet to the skin, and going on nerve alone. Not even Colonel Buse could explain it, but spontaneously those bedraggled and bedevilled Marines rose and charged that vertical face of rock and clay... That night we camped on the crest of Hill 660.'

On 16 January, a last Japanese counter-attack was repulsed and the battle for Cape Gloucester was over. Starving and sick, the remaining Japanese started pulling out of western New Britain towards Rabaul, which American forces finally captured by 20 March 1944.

BLOODY TARAWA

Meanwhile, the two-pronged attack across the Pacific was underway, with Tarawa Atoll in the Gilbert Islands as the first stop. The location of these islands was of great strategic significance, as they would serve as a springboard for the invasion of the Marshall and Caroline islands, important Japanese bases immediately to the north and west. Tarawa Atoll consists of a triangular necklace of flat coral islands, at the southwest corner of which lies Betio Island. About two miles in length, and never more than a half mile wide at any point, Betio is entirely ringed by a coral reef, and in 1943 was sheltered by palms and pandanus bushes.

Its Japanese garrison, commanded by Rear Admiral Meichi Shibasaki, consisted of 4,836 members of the Naval Guard Force, of whom 2,619 were elite Special Naval Landing troops. Offshore between the reefs and beaches was barbed wire, mines, and steel and concrete anti-boat obstacles designed to channel landing forces into the fire-lanes of the defenders ashore. Indeed, the Japanese shore defence system, which had been under construction since September 1942, consisted of a formidable array of armament, including 14 coast-defence guns ranging from 5.5-inch to 8-inch calibre, 25 concealed field guns, 14 tanks mounting 37 mm guns dug-in for static fire-power, 16 anti-aircraft guns, plus 106 pillboxes mainly containing 13 mm machine guns.

It was judged that a pre-D-day bombardment by the US Navy to soften these defences would have alerted the Japanese and pre-empted an enemy counter-strike. For the same reason, a Marine proposal that artillery be landed on the nearby unoccupied island of Bairiki was also rejected. Hence the forces allocated to the Tarawa portion of 'Operation Galvanic', composed of the 2nd Marine Division under Major General Julian C. Smith, were to go in 'cold'.

Regarding the reef barrier surrounding the island, Marine planners decided that the leading assault waves should use amphibious tractors (LVTs), but a mere 125 such vehicles, enough only for the first three assault waves, were available at that time! Subsequent support waves would have to be boated in. If these grounded on the razor-sharp coral, as the Raiders at Tulagi in the Solomons found earlier, men would have to wade the remaining 500 yards through chest deep water under fire. The most up-to-date tide chart of the Gilberts was over 100 years old, while recent information was contradictory. All available evidence pointed to the possibility that there would be five feet of water over the reef on the morning of D-day, but locals warned of a phenomenon called a 'dodging' or erratic tide, which could reduce

The Marines say: 'The difficult we do immediately. The impossible takes a little longer.' Here they prove it by laying a sandbag road under rough surf off the beach at Cape Gloucester. The 'Landing Ship, Tanks' carrying trucks, bulldozers, and other heavy vehicles and weapons, were unable to nose right up to the shore, and the 'SeaBees' and Coast Guardsmen, who manned the LSTs, had to lay the road for the equipment to drive onto the beach to aid in the capture of the airfield on Cape Gloucester.
Imperial War Museum Photo # NYF 14750

this depth considerably. A 'dodging tide' did indeed await the Marines on 20 November 1943.

The main landings were to take place on the least well-defended north, or lagoon, shore of the island, with the 2nd Marines, commanded by Colonel David Shoup, reinforced by the 2nd Battalion, 8th Marines, under Major Henry P. ("Jim") Crowe, comprising the first assault waves. This force was to be backed-up by one of the most advanced naval fire-support plans to date, which consisted of four battleships, two heavy cruisers, three light cruisers, and nine destroyers, under Rear Admiral Harry Hill. The landing force was assured that nothing would remain of the Japanese defences after the big naval guns had done their work. After the landings, General Holland Smith, 2nd Division commander, reminded those who predicted that the Marines would take Tarawa easily: 'Their only armor was a khaki shirt'!

Action began for the amphibious tractor crews during the early hours on D-day. Lieutenant Wallace Nygren, 2nd Amphibian Tractor Battalion recalled: 'We descended into the bowels of the LST [Landing Ship, Tank]. Seventeen LVTs waited there in the dimly lit hold. "Landing Vehicles Tracked." They loomed large and monstrous looking in the confines of the tank deck. We climbed aboard.

'Each Amtrac carried a regular crew of three. A driver, and assistant driver and a crew chief. As platoon leader, I was in the lead tractor with my maintenance sergeant, Tech. Sgt. Morris Wimer. We started the twin diesel Cadillac engines.

'Thirty four diesels roared into action. The noise was deafening. The tank deck filled with fumes from the exhausts. We waited—and waited. The ship continued to move and roll with a slow lazy roll. I felt, rather than heard, the ship's engines stop. Then the anchor chain rattled. We were at our station.

'Slowly the bow doors swung open and I could smell the tropic air. The upraised ramp in front of me fell forward into the water and there lay the dark and heaving ocean. Every crew chief stood tensed

on his gun platform watching me. I gave the arm signal, "Forward!"

'Tommy Kane, our crew chief, reached into the cab and signalled our driver. We climbed the small approach ramp and then rushed down the main ramp into the water. Correct timing was important. If you hit the ramp on the upward roll, it could break under the weight of the tractor.

'It was dark on the water. There were ships everywhere but only dimly seen. Not a light was showing. We made a wide swinging circle. The LST was spitting out Amtracs. We waited for them to join up. When all 17 were out, I motioned the direction we were to take and we plodded thru the water towards our troop ship. Our twin tracks scooped us along like a fat waddling duck. The rest of the platoon followed in single file. The tropic stars were brilliant but at the water level, visibility was poor. I knew where our ship was supposed to be. The huge armada of ships around us was more felt than seen. Our job was to pick up and land the troops of the second wave on Red Beach 2.'

Major Crowe had issued the following orders to his men on the evening before the assault: 'Carefully check all arms and equipment, especially first aid packs and gas masks. Be sure you have your ammunition — two full canteens and rations. Remember this may be all the ammunition, water

Above, keeping up the musical tradition of the Marines, the band of the 3rd Marine Division marches inland on Cape Gloucester in early 1943.
Imperial War Museum Photo # 21831

Next page, vehicles are driven and manhandled ashore at Cape Gloucester once the sandbag road has been laid. A 'Landing Vehicle, Tracked' (Mark 2), or 'Alligator', is followed by a jeep. Note the three Hospital Corpsmen carrying stretchers. Although Navy personnel, they wore Marine 'utilities' in combat.
Imperial War Museum Photo # 13041

and rations you will have for 24 to 48 hours. Do not *waste* it. Do not load weapons until ordered to do so. All packs and rolls must be made up. Clean all troop spaces thoroughly so there will be very little cleaning necessary on D day. Be sure you have a good pair of shoes to wear ashore.'

The *Time* magazine correspondent Bob Sherrod was with the men waiting aboard the troopships for the Amtracs, and recalled: 'By 03.30 the Marines had begun loading the outboard boats for the first wave. The sergeants were calling the roll: "Vernon, Simms, Gresholm…" They needed no light to call the well-remembered roll, and they didn't have to send a runner to find any absentees. The Marines were all there. One of the sergeants was giving his men last-minute instructions: "Be sure to correct your elevation and windage. Adjust your sights."

Bob Sherrod next watched outside the wardroom as the first and second waves walked through and out to their boats. He observed: 'Most of the men were soaked; their green-and-brown spotted jungle dungarees had turned a darker green when the sweat from their bodies soaked through. They jested with one another. Only a few even whistled to keep up their courage… They were a grimy, unshaven lot. The order had gone out: they must put on clean clothing just before going ashore, in order to diminish the chances of

infection from wounds, but now they looked dirty. Under the weight, light though it was, of their combat packs, lifebelts, guns, ammunition, helmets, canvas leggings, bayonets, they were sweating in great profusion. Nobody had shaved for two or three days.'

Suddenly a shell splashed into the water not more than 30 feet from an LST, indicating that the naval bombardment had not destroyed the big Japanese coastal guns. Aubrey K. Edmonds, an officer in the 8th Marines who landed in the first wave on Red Beach 3, recollected the moment when the LSTs were unexpectedly ordered away: 'After descending the cargo nets into the waiting landing boats we were almost immediately transferred into two amtracs, these being the only two available at that time. Our group had no sooner made the transfer when the transport, and all the other ships in the area, sailed away. Talk about a forlorn feeling!

'We knew something was wrong, but had no idea as to the cause of the convoy's sudden movement. We weren't sure if there had been a warning of an imminent surface attack or a prospective air or submarine attack. We were later told that the transport area had been too close to the landing beaches, and that several of the ships had been receiving shellfire from the Japanese defensive positions.'

As a result, those Amtracs which had not yet taken onboard their quota of Marines were forced to chase after the mother ships. By 0803 hours it became evident that the leading attack waves were well behind schedule. H-hour was twice delayed, first to 0845 and then to 0900, as the great mass of assault craft continued to jockey into their allocated stations. At this stage they came under ineffective fire from 75 mm air-burst plus a few machine guns. At 0854, and just six minutes away from H-hour, many of the Amtracs were still 15 minutes behind schedule. Nonetheless, Admiral Hill ordered covering fire from the big naval guns

Men of the 2nd Marine Division charge through Japanese crossfire to storm a heavily fortified enemy pill-box on Betio Island, Tarawa Atoll, during November 1943.
Imperial War Museum Photo # 10699

to cease, as originally planned, at 0855. As a result, during the ensuing quarter of an hour, the unprotected assault craft would close on the Betio beach without fire support.

The first Marines to go in were the 2nd Scout-Sniper Platoon led by First Lieutenant William Hawkins. Their job was to capture the long wooden pier which jutted out to the coral reef, and which bisected Red Beaches 2 and 3. Their Amtrac touched down at the edge of the reef at 0855, and Hawkins and five other men ran up the ramp, jumped on to the pier's end, and began to struggle through a pile of fuel drums dumped there to form a barrier. Met by a hail of Japanese small arms fire,

they waved the rest of the platoon to remain in the Amtrac while they advanced along the pier, wiping out the few remaining Japanese defenders with a flame-thrower!

BY THE RIGHT FLANK! EXECUTE

Meanwhile, the main assault waves started to approach the beach. Amtrac commander Lieutenant Nygren recalled: 'Finally, we began to move towards and parallel to the island. By 9 A.M. we were in position abreast of the beaches. Captain Lawrence gave the arm signal for all crew chiefs to relay back down the column. "By The Right Flank! Execute." Every arm went down and three long lines

A Marine dressed in first-pattern camouflage 'utilities', and draped with hand grenades and extra ammunition clips for his M1 rifle, rests on the beach after the fall of Tarawa, November 1943. His name, 'G. Newcomb', can be seen stencilled on the back of his pack.
Imperial War Museum Photo # 12204

of Amtracs, almost 100 in all, made a 90 degree right turn and three waves of tractors started moving towards the tiny island. We had been told by the naval gunfire liaison officers and Naval Air Force people that there would be no opposition left. I thought that they were overly optimistic. It was very bright now. The colors were deep and vivid. We were 1000 yards out from the island, in deep blue water. I could only see remnants of palm trees sticking up from low lying land. There were fires burning all along the shore. Black smoke welled up. The air was filled with wisps of burnt powder bags from our naval rifles. The air smelled burned. The sun blazed down and it was getting very warm... I could see the water ahead breaking over the fringing coral reef. The reef water was green in color, indicating its shallowness. Then we were over it. The tractors lurched and tossed as we climbed the coral heads. The troops in our open compartment were thrown about. Our 3 neat lines became ragged as we bounced and lumbered along the reef. Mortar shells from shore began to explode around us.'

Soon after the US naval bombardment lifted, the Japanese opened fire. Crouching low in his Amtrac, Aubrey Edmonds, 8th Marines, observed: 'As we got within 1,000 yards of the beach we opened fire with both the forward "50s" [machine guns] as well as our 30 mms mounted aft. Our guns took a heavy toll of the Japs on the pier as we hit the beach.'

PFC Robert J. Reder, 2nd Battalion, 2nd Marines, remembered: 'The last few minutes in the Amtrac were a jumble of sensations: Mortar and artillery fire rocking the Amtrac with geysers of water; the Amtrac bouncing over the coral reef; machine gun fire ricocheting off its armored sides; torpedo bombers and Hellcats streaking overhead to bomb and strafe the island, and then the shout: "'Let's Go!'"

The first battalion lost 10 per cent casualties before reaching Red Beach 1, while the following battalions sustained about 20 per cent casualties in the water. Lieutenant Al Tidwell, 8th Marines, was in an assault wave guide boat heading towards Red Beach 3, east of the pier, and recalled: 'My platoon of 41-plus men, had eighteen dead and three wounded before getting our feet on the sand... Going in to the beach at Tarawa, I angled toward the pier. It looked like it might protect me from at least one angle. Me and a few of my men had made it to where the water was less than knee deep. Immediately behind me a man got shot and dropped.'

The man hit was PFC Pruitt. After lying there in the water for a few minutes, Pruitt shoved his hand through his dungarees to check for blood, only to find the bullet had passed through his BAR

ammunition belt and hit a magazine which caused a few bullets to explode harmlessly!

WE HAVE NOTHING LEFT TO LAND

Approaching Red Beach 2 in the centre, Lieutenant Colonel Herbert R. Amey, Jr., commander of the 2nd Battalion, 2nd Marines, had less luck. Killed in the water by a burst of enemy machine gun fire, he was replaced by Lieutenant Colonel W. I. Jordan, an observer from the 4th Marine Division. Of the moment he hit the beach, Robert Reder recollected: 'As I went over the side, the weight on my back threw me off balance, and I landed with my face in the sand. I raised my head, saw the coconut log seawall we had been told about, then watched a wounded Marine half-dive and half-roll from the top to the sand of the beach.

'Fear took over. This was real! I looked toward the sea. About half of the first three waves of Amtracs had made it to shore and were depositing their frightened cargoes. The rest were strewn on the reef and beach, surrounded by bodies.'

Reder was probably looking across towards the 3rd Battalion, 2nd Marines, many of whom were still stuck in their vehicles beyond the reef off Red Beach 1. Ordered by Colonel Shoup to change plans and land his men on Red 2, battalion commander Major John Schoettel radioed back: 'We have nothing left to land.'

The 8th Marines had greater success. Lieutenant Edmonds commanded one of two Amtracs which found a breach in the coconut log seawall near the base of the pier, and dashed through to unload their Marines near the airstrip. He recalled: 'My tractor did not disembark troops on the beach, but went through the bunkers and first line of beach defenses, disembarking on the taxi-way. We immediately moved on to the main airstrip. There we set up our machine gun along with our line of fire that had been designated as our first objective. I would estimate that we had organized our lines in not more than twenty minutes.'

Back on the beach, Staff Sergeant William J. Bordelon, Jr., of the division engineers, 18th Marines, plus two men, struggled ashore after their Amtrac received a direct hit while crossing the coral, killing all but five of its occupants. Hastily making up demolition charges, Bordelon rolled over the sea wall and knocked out two Japanese pillboxes, before receiving an arm wound. Undeterred, he crawled toward a third pillbox before being severely wounded by machine gun fire. Refusing medical aid, he picked up a rifle and gave covering fire to Marines scaling the seawall. Cries for help from wounded comrades drew him back to the blood-stained seawater, where he dragged to shore a wounded demolition expert plus another man who had been badly hit trying to rescue the engineer. Going on to destroy a fourth pillbox with a rifle grenade, he finally received a fatal wound. For his amazing bravery under fire, William Bordelon, Jr. was posthumously awarded the Medal of Honor.

Out at sea, the Higgins boats of the fourth wave began to stall on the coral reef which the 'dodging tide' quickly exposed. PFC Jeremiah Hanafin, M Company, 3rd Battalion, 6th Marines, remembered: 'Without any warning our Higgins boat slammed into the reef. As the craft ground to a halt, our Coast Guard driver lowered the front ramp

and hollered, "This is as far as I go!" We charged out into the surf, which I quickly discovered came right up to my chest. It was then I got my first clear view of Tarawa. What a mess! Holding my M-1 carbine and two boxes of 30 caliber machine gun ammo over my head, my singular thought was to get to the beach. I just followed the guy in front of me... As I waded in closer to the beach my nose and throat became filled with the smell of death.'

Major Robert Voorhees, 3rd Battalion, 8th Marines, recollected: '...our "K" Company in Higgins boats were dumped on submerged reefs left of the pier, and about 800 yards from "Red Beach Three" area. As a Higgins boat's ramp

Their M1s ready for action, Marines leap from an LVT(2), or Amtrac, onto the beach to join waiting assault squad members at one of the islands in Kwajalein atoll in the Marshall Islands. Amtracs could carry between 20 to 24 fully equipped troops, or a cargo upwards of three tons. They could approach the beaches at a maximum of four knots, and were capable of speeding up to 25 m.p.h. once they hit dry land. The reason why this vehicle has stopped at the waters edge is probably because it was under orders to return across the coral reef to pick up and land more Marines. *Imperial War Museum Photo # 18661*

splashed down on the surf, [PFC] Clarence Boersma, with his light air-cooled .306 calibre Browning automatic machine gun, leaped in five foot of water... reeled back, and sinking over his head in water, instinctively walked on the bottom of the ocean floor towards the direction of the pier, which was about 300 feet to his right and front, until his head was above water. With weapon in hand, he marched on, angling towards the pier and defying the bullets that skimmed on all around him. But, again, he sank this time in about ten feet of water, hitting bottom. He pushed off the reef with his feet bobbing upward for air and repeating this until he reached the left side of the pier. About a hundred yards down along the pier he looked up to his right side to see D. L. Ulrich on top of the pier moving toward the shore.

"Ulrich, take my machine gun and I will join you," yelled Clarence.

'Exhausted, Clarence pulled himself up onto the pier, stood up and took... an apple out of his back pocket. He bit into the apple between heaving desperately for air, apparently oblivious to shells bursting into boats laden with marines and to the noise from chattering machine gun fire of the enemy from the left flank searching out marines, young men, moving thru floating bodies in bloody water; with deadly accurate sniper fire coming from beneath the pier by the searamp area finding its targets.

"Where else can you get a dollar a day, go for a morning swim and eat an apple," remarked Clarence to Ulrich.'

By midday, the assault had ground to a halt with many exhausted Marines still pinned down on the 20-foot wide beaches. Reinforcements reached them painfully slowly. Some of those men stuck on the coral reef in Higgins boats were picked up by Amtracs whose crews bravely risked their lives transferring them closer to the beach. By this time, Colonel Shoup had come ashore, but his command

post was only 15 feet inland. All that afternoon, small groups of Marines punched away at the Japanese pillboxes with hand grenades, demolition charges, and flamethrowers. Elsewhere, riflemen attempted to charge over the log sea wall in order to kill their tormentors, only to be mowed down by relentless machine gun fire. Companies I and K, 3rd Battalion, 2nd Marines, lost half their men in two hours in such an attempt. Realising the desperate nature of the situation, Shoup sent for reinforcements.

By nightfall, of the 5,000 Marines huddled in two shallow enclaves along the northwestern beach at Betio, 1,500 lay dead or wounded. Expecting a Japanese counterattack that night, the survivors dug foxholes in the sand. Under cover of darkness, artillery personnel of the 10th Marines lugged 75mm pack howitzer pieces ashore on their backs, while water and ammunition were carried along the pier.

Mercifully, the Japanese attack did not materialise. With his communication system destroyed by pre-invasion naval bombardment, Admiral Shibasaki was unable to gather sufficient forces and missed a valuable opportunity to push the Marines back off the island. As a result, the latter were able to consolidate their position. At dawn the next day, the corps reserve began its

Two Marines, members of a Fleet Marine Force communications unit operating with amphibious landing forces on Kwajalein Atoll in the Marshall Islands, set up a field telephone on a wreck-strewn beach during action on Roi-Namur, one of the islands in the atoll. Radios used by the Marines were low-power sets. The TBX had little range and the TBY frequently failed when it got wet! *Imperial War Museum Photo # 16578*

landing, and also met with heavy losses as men of
the 6th Marines, plus the 1st Battalion, 8th Marines,
came ashore. Concentrating on the more lightly
defended western tip of the island, two battalions
of the 6th Marines managed to link up with
remnants of the 2nd Marines, under Major Michael
P. Ryan. Bunker by bunker, other battalions began
to converge, as the fire-power of the 10th Marine
howitzers took its toll. By the afternoon of the
second day, Shoup was at last able to inform
General Smith that the tide of battle had turned:
'Casualties many. Percentage dead not known.
Combat efficiency—we are winning.'

The gap was finally closed between the two
beaches on the third day, during which First
Lieutenant Alexander Bonnyman, Jr, 2nd Battalion,
8th Marines, who had already shown extreme
bravery, gave up his life taking the Japanese
strongpoint east of the wharf virtually single-
handed. During the fourth day, the 6th Marines
overran the island's eastern tip, while the remainder
of the force mopped up the survivors. Total Marine
casualties on Betio amounted to 3,318 Americans,
of which 1,085 died. Of the 146 prisoners taken
on the island, only 17 were Japanese soldiers—
the rest were Korean labourers.

The bloody nature of the battle for Tarawa
shocked the American nation, and many
questioned the value of frontal assault against
well-defended island strongholds. Nonetheless,
lessons were learned. Air and naval support fire
needed to be more methodical and accurate.
The landing force needed many more LVTs to
cross the coral reefs. Communications between
landing forces and support fire needed vast
improvement. These things would come in time,
but for the present the Marines turned their
attention to more immediate matters.

The next stop was Kwajalein, an atoll in the
Marshall Islands. The V Amphibious Corps assault
force for 'Operation Flintlock' consisted of the
4th Marine and 7th Army Divisions. This time the
Marine landings, which took place on 31 January
1944, were preceded by a two-day bombardment,
plus shelling from nearby islands and rockets from
new LCI-gunboats. Despite a continued shortage
of Amtracs to get into the coral-ringed lagoon,
the 23rd, 24th, and 25th Marines took five small,
poorly defended islands, including Ennubirr,
Obella, and Roi/Namur in two days at a cost of
313 dead and 502 wounded. The Army received
slightly fewer casualties taking the larger island
of Kwajalein between 1-4 February 1944.

Success at Kwajalein was a great source of
encouragement to the planners. Employing the
V Amphibious Corps reserve, composed of the

22nd Marines and two battalions of the 106th
Infantry, General T. E. Watson was ordered to
move on quickly to capture Eniwetok Atoll. D-day
was 17 February—less than three weeks after
the original landings in the Marshall Islands.
Eniwetok was a tougher nut to crack, and it took
over a thousand Marine and Army casualties
to achieve it, as the Japanese took to their
underground 'spider web' defences, and sniped
at advancing Marines and GIs.

THE MARIANA ISLANDS

Having secured the Marshall Islands, the US
advance across the Pacific gathered momentum.
Joint Chiefs of Staff decided that General
MacArthur would push on through New Guinea to
the Philippines, while Admiral Nimitz would invade
the Mariana Islands. The capture of the latter
location would bring Japan and the Philippines
within striking distance of the Army Air Forces'
new B-29 bombers. The three islands in the
Marshalls selected for invasion were Saipan,
Tinian, and Guam, which also lay across the lines
of supply and communication between Japan
and conquered territories in Malaya and the
Dutch East Indies. If these lines could be cut, it
would inflict heavy damage on Japan's economy
and military capabilities.

Furthermore, Saipan was the headquarters of
the Japanese Central Pacific Fleet, being defended
by 29,662 troops, including a tank regiment, an
anti-aircraft regiment, and two engineer regiments.
The US task force designated for its capture
consisted of some 800 ships and 162,000
Marines and GIs, all of which was to be protected
by Admiral Raymond Spruance's Fifth Fleet. This
Joint Expeditionary Force was under the overall
command of Vice Admiral Kelly Turner, with General
Holland Smith commanding the Marines. The Army
27th Infantry Division was held in reserve, while
another Army division stood by in Hawaii.

The Marines hit the beach at Charan Kanoa, near
the Aslito airfield, in Saipan, on 15 June 1944.
Engineer officer G. L. H. Cooper recalled the
morning of the attack: 'I doubt that many of us had
slept a great deal during the night, and all of us
who were not otherwise occupied were out on deck
looking at the dim outline of the island rimmed with
little fires from earlier bombardments. Before dawn
we had our usual steak and eggs, had our gear all
ready, boat teams were standing by, landing craft
were in the water, and, despite the usual shipboard
noises and orders being given, everything seemed
unnaturally quiet. This was our biggest operation—
two Marine divisions landing abreast over beaches
called Red, Blue, Green and Yellow... And there was

another one of those damned reefs.'

PFC Jeremiah Hanafin, 3rd Battalion, 6th Marines, remembered: 'Knowing I was in the first assault wave didn't cause me any nightmares. I can't remember getting any premonitions about being killed. Besides, you can't do an effective job if you're constantly worried and trying to avoid danger. That kind of attitude will force you to compromise your duties and responsibilities. Discipline saw us through—discipline gained from training. You just do your best, trust in God, and keep believing you'll get home.'

According to Technical Sergeant Pete Zurlinden: 'After breakfast, the Marines remain topside to watch the naval blasting. They are quiet, laconic in their conversation. Somewhat later the troops are ordered below to their compartments to pull on their combat gear. Characteristically, most of them say at one time or other while slipping into their packs. "Well, this is it!"

'Then comes the command, resonantly rolling through the ship's public address system: "Lower all boats!" It's the Leathernecks' show from now on.'

The first assault waves consisting of four Marine regiments were led in by 24 LCI-gunboats, or amphibious tanks, blasting away with their 75mm howitzers and rocket launchers. Aboard the crowded Amtracs were the veterans of Tarawa and the Marshall Islands. As they approached the reef, the gunboats turned clear, and the armoured amphibians, or LVT(A)s, opened fire with their 37 mm guns, backed up by the 50 calibre machine guns on the lead wave of 96 Amtracs, raising a pall of smoke and dust over the island as their shells and bullets crashed into the Jap defence works.

The moment the LVTs bellied over the coral, the reef appeared to explode in a torrent of deadly accurate enemy artillery and mortar fire which scored numerous direct hits. Within 20 minutes, 8,000 Marines were ashore. The 6th and 8th Marines landed 900 yards too far north, and suffered heavy casualties, including all four assault commanders. The 6th Marines were halted 400 yards inland and, by midday 35 per cent of this regiment was either dead or wounded.

A survivor of this onslaught, PFC Hanafin, recollected: 'Our craft ground its way over the intervening reef and continued shoreward. Once we hit the beach we didn't advance in very far. The Amtrac stopped and we jumped over the sides with our equipment. I had the machine gun; the thing must have weighed 50 lbs. "Speed" [the first gunner] had the tripod. No one had to say, "Let's go!" We just leapt out. It was instinct. What else could you do? If you stayed there you were a sitting target.

'Confusion was rampant. We were half in the water, laying there waiting for orders. Artillery and mortar shells were zeroing in all around us. Nothing seemed right. The landmarks were unfamiliar. We had landed north of our proposed beaches because of the murderous anti-boat fire.

'Finally we received orders to move inland. We worked our way in maybe a hundred yards when "Speed" put down the tripod and I slammed down the gun on top of it. He adjusted it and I fed in the belts of ammo. My job was to keep feeding while "Speed" kept firing.'

PFC Clarence E. Hargis, 2nd Battalion, 6th Marines, recalled his landing experience,

Opposite, Marines toss hand grenades toward a suspected enemy stronghold on Saipan during July/August 1944. Once the safety lever had been released, the three-second fuse gave the man little time to act.
Imperial War Museum Photo # 30649

Above, the first Marines ashore dig-in after landing on the beach at Saipan. An Amtrac burns in the background after a direct hit from enemy shell-fire.
Imperial War Museum Photo # NYF 30330

and the inevitable counterattack of General Yoshitsugu Saito's forces: 'We were taking a hell of a pounding by Japanese mortars and artillery shells. There wasn't a safe place on the beach. A buddy of mine and I had taken cover in a big shell hole which we thought was the best cover we could find for the night. Things were getting really tough. After awhile my buddy, William Chisler, made the remark that he thought we should take different cover. I reluctantly moved to another position with him. At 10 p.m. the bugles sounded and the Japs frantically attacked Fox Company's lines, coming down and beside the beach road. The first banzai was repelled. The bugles blew again at 2 a.m., hitting Fox Company's lines again. This attack again was repelled. The bugles again sounded at 4 a.m., and they came charging down the left flank on the beach trying frantically to break our lines and through to the command post. We suffered very heavy casualties. The situation on the left flank was in doubt, but we succeeded in holding. I think the approximate count of Japanese in front of Fox Company's lines was five to seven hundred. Most of them were in stacks of eight to ten bodies as they were using their dead for cover. As my buddy and I were surveying the beach the next morning after daybreak, he motioned for me to come there. He was standing over the shell hole that we had first used for cover.

I looked in the shell hole and saw two Marines. They had taken a direct hit by a mortar or artillery shell. I never knew their names or who they were. I asked Chisler what possessed him to want to move from that position to another. All I could ever get from him was that "something kept telling me to get out of this hole." That one didn't seem to have our names on it. "God Bless the two Marines" and all the others who paid the supreme sacrifice for Fox Company...'

Elsewhere that night, the 1st Battalion, 6th Marines, was hit by 44 Japanese tanks. The Marines, mostly riflemen, fought back bravely, and PFC Robert S. Creed of Cabot, Arkansas, stopped four tanks with his M1A1 rocket launcher, after which he climbed on board a fifth tank and dropped in a grenade. Another bazooka team knocked out seven more tanks. Only a dozen of the vehicles survived, while more than 300 Jap soldiers lay dead. By 0700 hours, the assault was crushed.

According to Jeremiah Hanafin: 'Once the sun came up we thought it was over. The Japanese would go into defensive positions during the day while we took the offensive. I was sitting there taking a breather, smoking my pipe. As I glanced to my left, in the direction of a long trench, I noticed something moving toward our gun. It was a Jap wearing a camouflage helmet. He'd crawl,

Marines turn the fire of a captured Japanese mountain gun on enemy positions in Garapan, the capital of Saipan in 1944. One Marine with field glasses watches the results of the fire, while another holds his ears against the explosion. *Imperial War Museum Photo # 30631*

stop, lift his head, then crawl a little more… So I took the gun and swung it over. The next time that Jap lifted his head, it was sayonara. I just kept firing and he kept bouncing.'

The Marines needed reinforcements and during the night of 17-18 June, the 27th Infantry Division came ashore. The GIs took a position on the 4th Marine Division's right flank, and helped take the Aslito airfield. By 20 June, US forces had cleared most of the southern end of Saipan, although the extreme southern tip of the island remained a warren of concealed caves and bunkers occupied by Japanese survivors. On 1 July, the 2nd Marine Division captured what was left of Garapan, bringing Tanapag Harbor into American hands. The expected Japanese banzai charge finally came on 7 July, when 2,500 Japanese troops charged down on elements of the Infantry Division, who broke and fell back in confusion. This attack was finally halted when Marine artillery of the 3rd Battalion, 10th Marines, cut their fuses and fired their howitzers at virtually point blank range into the enemy. 'The Japs came at us four abreast', said one gunner, 'We fired 105s into the ground 50 feet in front of us.' According to *Time* correspondent Bob Sherrod, who surveyed the scene the next day: 'The whole area seemed to be a mass of stinking bodies, spilled guts, and brains.'

Two days later, General Holland Smith declared the island secured. The loss of Saipan, combined with the Battle of the Philippine Sea, or 'Marianas Turkey Shoot', during which the Japanese First Mobile Fleet was destroyed, brought down the Japanese premier, Hideki Tojo, who finally resigned on 18 July, 1944. General Saito, who had ordered the last banzai attack on the island, committed *hara-kiri*. Vice Admiral Chuichi Nagumo, who had led the attack on Pearl Harbor, and who was now commander of the no longer existing First Mobile Fleet, shot himself in the head. Only 1,000 of the Japanese on Saipan survived. The rest were either killed in battle, or committed suicide by leaping from the cliffs! The bloody 25-day struggle for Saipan had cost 3,426 American dead and 13,099 wounded. Japanese dead were estimated at over 32,800. Although it was a costly battle, one Japanese admiral declared, 'Our war was lost with the loss of Saipan.' Marine commander General Holland Smith described it as 'the decisive battle of the Pacific offensive'.

THE PERFECT AMPHIBIOUS OPERATION

Only three miles across the water from Saipan lies Tinian, a symmetrical, green island dominated by Mount Lasso, and ringed by sharp coral cliffs. Its three small air strips, lying among what amounted to one large cane field, were ideally suited for B 29 runways. However, its three beaches, two in the northwestern coast and a larger one at Tinian Town —a ramshackle village built around a sugar mill in the south, offered the planners little scope for amphibious assault. Colonel Kiyochi Ogata's defence works consisted of a powerful system of coastal batteries manned and supported by a 9,162-strong garrison. His heaviest fortifications were installed behind the Tinian Town beach, on the assumption that this would be the main point of attack. The other two beaches were, by normal convention, too narrow — one being only 160 yards wide, and the other a mere 60 yards. Hence, Ogata had placed only a few machine guns and anti-boat guns there, and no mines.

While planning the attack, General Holland Smith concluded: 'If we go in at Tinian Town, we'll have another Tarawa.' Thus, on 24 July 1944, the 2nd and 4th Marine Divisions created a diversion off Tinian Town, while landing on the two smaller, narrower beaches. This took the Japanese completely by surprise. As such, the assault on northwestern Tinian represented the perfect amphibious operation. The landings were preceded by a systematic naval, artillery, and air bombardment, the latter involving the first use of napalm, a fearsome concoction of jellied fuel oil and petrol dropped in large fire-bombs by close-support aircraft.

On J-day, the 24th Marines, 4th Division, came rushing ashore in column of battalion on White Beach 1, while two battalions of the 25th Marines landed abreast on White Beach 2. Every serviceable Amtrac in V Corps, amounting to 533 vehicles, was made available for the operation. Marine riflemen left their packs behind, taking nothing but their weapons, ammunition, poncho, a spoon, and a bottle of mosquito repellent. Artillery was restricted to pack howitzers, while heavier 105 mm and 155 mm guns gave support fire from nearby Saipan.

According to Major F. E. Garretson, the landings were 'a cake walk'. The 24th Marines' assault company moved swiftly off White 1 beach, although last-minute mines, potholes, and coral heads slowed progress down somewhat on White 2. By evening, 15,614 Marines were ashore and in possession of all main objectives, at a cost of 15 killed and 225 wounded. Despite vicious counterattacks that night, the Japanese failed to dislodge the Americans. During further advances the next day, the 4th Marine Division secured Mount Lasso and Ushi Airdrome.

Engineer officer G. L. H. Cooper recalled the moment the Marines ran into stiff enemy resistance

Dressed in his war paint, the Marine in plain jacket is probably an Amtrac crewman. Nosing into the beach at Guam, he manages to smile for cameraman Corporal Martin J. McEvilly, Jr. The black smudging on his face helped his vision by killing the reflection from his skin, and was an asset both at sea and ashore because an upturned white face was clearly visible to pilots of enemy aircraft. *Imperial War Museum Photo # HU75666*

inland: 'We had been stopped before but never, as I recall, so suddenly or completely — we just couldn't get into, let alone through, that damned cane field. We tried wetting down the face of the cliff with a tank mounted flame thrower, and we tried our little 37 mm pop guns and mortars, but the Japanese fire continued. We called for artillery and air support but for some reason or other this request could not be granted. We couldn't move forward so we established a line in the woods to harass the cliff while the unit on our flank moved in to try to locate a better way of getting up the blasted thing. They succeeded a bit better than did we and, when trying to clean out the cliff side pockets from above, found that the Japanese had pulled out.'

J. Fred Haley, 1st Battalion, 8th Marines, encountered stiffer resistance as his unit fought its way to the top of the cliffs: 'As the 2d and 3d Platoons of Company A proceeded across the plateau on a line of skirmishes, we were suddenly hit by automatic fire and fire coming from a tree-line that formed the southeast border of the canefield to our front. The cane had been reduced to stubble and didn't afford much protection or camouflage. After hitting the ground, I noticed an abandoned Japanese gun tub containing an anti-aircraft gun pointing skyward about 100 to 150 feet to my left. Running with "all engines full ahead" I dove over the

top into that sandbagged gun emplacement. Already occupying this somewhat tattered and torn gun fortification was a bazooka operator and a corporal whom I knew to be from New York, both from the 3d Platoon.

'The Japanese were ricocheting bullets off the barrel of the anti-aircraft gun, some of which were coming uncomfortably close to us as we tried to make ourselves as small as possible inside the gun tub. The New Yorker, a cool and resourceful Marine, fired several rounds from his MI rifle into two closed wooden doors at the ground level of the gun tub, blowing open the doors and revealing two armed Japanese soldiers who had been hiding in the ammunition storage compartment. It was an impulsive act on the corporal's part: he heard a noise in the compartment and instinctively fired into it. He not only blew the doors open but he killed the Japanese occupants. We might well have been killed too, had there been ammunition inside.'

The Japanese banzai attack finally came at dawn the next day. According to Haley: 'They came at our half circle from all sides; several attempted to clamber up the cliff from our right rear. But we were not to be denied. We had struggled long and hard to gain a foothold on that plateau at the top of the cliff and we clung to it as though our lives depended on it, which indeed they did. 2d Battalion never did reach the top of the cliff, but somehow managed to form a connecting line... and this helped in great measure to protect our rear during the night.

'By sunup the Japanese had shot their bolt and the battle for Tinian was history. They were stacked outside our perimeter in numbers somewhere between 100 and 200. I remember the names painted on the water-jackets of two of our .30 caliber water-cooled Browning machineguns that accounted for most of these Japanese bodies: on one jacket was painted the inscription "Ice Cold Katie" and on the other "Hot Pants".'

By 30 July, Tinian Town had fallen and by 1 August 1944, the whole island was in US hands.

Marine-laden Higgins boats move in for the attack on Peleliu, in the Palau Islands. The shore is shrouded in smoke from Japanese installations hit by warships and planes of US Admiral William F. Halsey's Third Fleet. The veteran campaigners of the famed 1st Marine Division, fondly known as the 'Old Breed', hacked out a mile and a half of beachhead on 15 September 1944.
Imperial War Museum Photo # NYF 40128

General Holland Smith declared subsequently: 'Tinian was the perfect amphibious operation in the Pacific War'!

OPERATION STEVEDORE

The recapture of Guam, which a 153-man Marine garrison had surrendered to the Japanese on 10 December 1941, was a long-standing American ambition, and a well-practised exercise at the Marine Corps School at Quantico, Virginia. One hundred miles farther south, Guam was ten miles longer, five miles wider, and three times larger than Saipan. After a fierce 17-day bombardment, 'Operation Stevedore' swung into action on

21 July 1944, and the 3rd Marine Division, plus the 1st Provisional Marine Brigade, under overall command of Major General Roy Geiger, took to their assault craft after a frustrating 50-day wait in the broiling Pacific heat.

The landings on Agat beach were difficult. The Orote Peninsula, site of the old Marine barracks, separated the two landing beaches, which were defended by 18,500 Japanese soldiers under Lieutenant General Takeshi Takashina. Enemy resistance, mainly from two anti-boat guns in a concrete block house on Gaan Point, was vicious. Twenty-four Amtracs were hit or sunk by mines, while reefs prevented surviving craft getting

Above, in this aerial view, landing craft carrying the Marines of the First Division can be seen streaking toward the beaches, while heavy naval bombardment from vessels offshore covers the whole island of Peleliu with a blanket of smoke and flame.
Imperial War Museum Photo # NYF 41612

Next page, Marine war artist Harry Reeks was one of a six-man public relations team sent to cover the invasion of Iwo Jima in 1945. In this dramatic study, Reeks depicts the rough seas which hampered the Iwo landings. The open doors of a 'Landing Ship, Tank' are seen to the left, with Amtracs emerging into the ocean.
Anne S. K. Brown Military Collection

right up to the beach. According to one rifleman, this gave the Marines 'a long wade to the beach, searching for footing on the treacherous coral bottom, wrestling with their equipment, sometimes to their necks in water'.

The main objective once ashore was Mount Alifan, which by the following evening had been scaled and captured, whilst further advances took place along the Orote Peninsula. On the evening of 25 July, the Japanese launched the most massive counterattack of the war to date. The Marine front line on the northern beachhead extended five miles and leaked like a 'sieve', as Japanese loaded down with explosives and land mines ran through, and blew themselves up in the process! Some broke through to a field hospital, where wounded Marines, dressed only in their skivvies, beat them off! In the sector held by the 1st Battalion, 21st Marines, 50 men of B Company were destroyed in one of these suicide attacks. The hardest hit was the 2nd Battalion, 9th Marines, who withstood seven major assaults from the *sake*-soaked Japanese. Captain Louis H. Wilson, Jr., F Company, had been wounded three times the previous day. Hearing the renewed noise of battle, he left the medical aid station and rejoined his command. All night long he led his men in hand-to-hand fighting, and at one point dashed 50 yards under enemy fire to rescue

A Marine assault squad takes cover behind an Amtrac on the Peleliu beach during landings of 15 September 1944. The man at centre wearing a plain steel helmet is probably a radio operator. In the face of fierce Japanese resistance, the men of the 1st Marine Division eventually seized an airfield and had virtually split the Peleliu defense in half four days after landing. *Imperial War Museum Photo # NYP 39611*

a wounded Marine. He next scaled a nearby slope and, although losing 13 of his 17-man patrol, managed to capture a critical area of high ground in front of his lines. Wilson was one of four Marines to be awarded the Medal of Honor for bravery under fire on Guam.

After three days of further bitter fighting, the Japanese commander was killed, and the 22nd Marines reached the old barracks and went on to capture Orote airfield. The following afternoon, 'To the Colors' was blown on a captured Japanese bugle amidst the ruins of the old Marine parade ground, and the American flag was officially raised on Guam for the first time since 10 December 1941.

MEANINGLESS BATTLE

Most wars produce a meaningless battle, and Peleliu in the Palaus Islands, scene of Colonel Ellis' mysterious death in 1923, amounted to that battle in the Pacific. The original plan was to commence MacArthur's campaign to retake the Philippines by landing on the island of Mindanao, but Peleliu would also have to be captured in order to secure the American right flank. Meanwhile, Admiral Halsey, who was operating near the Philippines, advised that Leyte, to the north, was not as well defended. Leyte was indeed chosen as the invasion point, but the Marines were still sent in to take Peleliu, and no one realised how well it was defended.

Peleliu marked a change in enemy defensive tactics. No longer were the Japanese prepared to make an all-out stand on the beaches and, when that failed, die in a drunken *banzai* charge. On Peleliu, the 10,700 defenders, commanded by Colonel Kumio Nakagawa, somehow managed to hack their way into the rock-hard coral hills, thereby forming a network of interconnected gunposts and machine gun nests. They would allow the Marines to get ashore, and then punish them dearly.

General Rupertus' 1st Marine Division, in action

again after a miserable period of 'rest and recreation' in the dampness and humidity of Pavuvu in the Solomons, began the aptly-named 'Operation Stalemate' at 0830 hours on 15 September 1944. All three of his infantry regiments were to land abreast over five wide beaches on the southwest shore of Peleliu. The 5th Marines, commanded by Colonel 'Bucky' Harris, would hit the centre beach with Peleliu's airstrip as its main objective. Two battalions of the 7th Marines, under Colonel 'Haiti' Hanneken, would cover the right flank to secure the island's southern tip. The 1st Marines, led by Colonel 'Chesty' Puller, had the hardest job. Landing on the left flank, they were to wheel left and capture the Umurbrogol ridges to the north.

The three-day preliminary bombardment proved largely ineffective against the underground Japanese bunkers. As the first assault wave hit the coral reef, all hell let loose as shell fire and mortar bombs screamed into the crowded Amtracs. A chaplain who went in with the Marines recalled: 'How we got through the murderous mortar fire which the Japs were laying down on the reef we'll never know. The bursts were everywhere and our men were being hit, left and right.'

Twenty-six Amtracs received direct hits during this action, while all of the 30 tanks unloaded with the fourth assault wave were destroyed. On the right, the 7th Marines ran into a hornet's nest of unscathed defence works, including minefields, pillboxes, a blockhouse, plus anti-boat guns which enfiladed the shore line. Major E. H. Hurst, the lead battalion commander, managed to find shelter in an anti-tank ditch, from where he re-grouped his shattered command and pushed inland.

In the centre, the 5th Marines found only light resistance, and advanced swiftly across the southern part of the airfield, thereby securing its position before nightfall. Meanwhile, the 1st Marines hit the Umurbrogol. This series of coral ridges lay immediately behind the beach, and was bristling with pillboxes and machine gun nests.

The historian of the 1st Marines described the terrain before them as 'the worst ever encountered by the regiment in three Pacific campaigns. Along its centre the rocky spine was heaved up in a contorted mass of decayed coral, strewn with rubble, crags, ridges and gulches thrown together in a confusing maze… It was impossible to dig in: the best a man could do was to pile a little coral or wood debris round their positions. The jagged rock slashed their shoes and clothes, and tore their bodies every time they hit the deck for safety.'

Another Marine facing the Umurbrogol recorded: 'Casualties were higher for the simple reason it was impossible to get under the ground away from the Japanese mortar barrages. Each blast hurled chunks of coral in all directions, multiplying many times the fragmentation effect of every shell.'

Jutting out on the beach to their left was a bastion of coral which cost Captain George P. Hunt, commanding K Company, 1st Marines, two-thirds of his men. Hunt observed: 'The Point, rising 30 feet above the water's edge, was of solid, jagged coral, a rock-mass of sharp pinnacles, deep crevasses, tremendous boulders. Pillboxes, reinforced with steel and concrete, had been dug or blasted in the base of the perpendicular drop to the beach. Others, with coral and concrete piled six feet on top, were constructed above, and spider holes were

Marines using rifle grenades and Molotov cocktails engaging the Japanese who were well-entrenched in caves on 'Suicide Ridge', Peleliu. One sof the men is about to throw his flaming missile at the enemy. In the centre is the torch used to light the 'cocktails'. The men on 'Suicide Ridge' fought for nine days before relief arrived and they could go to a rear base. *Imperial War Museum Photo # 75667*

blasted around them for protecting infantry. It surpassed by far anything we had conceived of when we studied the aerial photographs.'

Hitting this position from the rear, Hunt and what was left of his riflemen, seized and held the crest of the Point, but were cut off when the Japanese counterattacked. When advised that his company commander was low on ammunition and down to 18 men, Colonel Puller commented: 'That's fine. Tell him to keep pushing!'

During the next three days, the 1st Marines, joined by the 7th Marines, fought their way up the Umurbrogol in temperatures that sometimes reached a searing 110 degrees Fahrenheit. The *Time* magazine reporter, Robert Martin, wrote: 'Pelelieu is a horrible place. The heat is stifling and rain falls intermittently — the muggy rain that brings no relief, only greater misery. The coral rocks soak up the heat during the day and it is only slightly cooler at night. Marines... wilted on Pelelieu. By the 4th day there were as many casualties from heat prostration as from wounds.'

Hill 210 was eventually taken on 18 September. PFC Russell Davis, a scout with the 1st Marines, later recalled of this action: 'As the riflemen climbed higher they grew fewer, until only a handful of men still climbed in the lead squads. These were the pick of the bunch—the few men who would go forward, no matter what was ahead. There were only a few. Of the thousands who land with a division and the hundreds who go up with a company line, there are only a few who manage to live and have enough courage to go through anything. They are the bone structure of a fighting outfit. All the rest is so much weight and sometimes merely flab. There aren't more than a few dozen in every thousand men, even in the Marines. They clawed and clubbed and stabbed their way up. The rest of us watched. Watching them go up, Buck, the old rifleman, said, "Take a look at that sight and remember it. Those are riflemen, boy, and there ain't many like them. I was one once."'

The carnage on Peleliu continued amidst bombs and flame-throwers in the caves and coral ridges, as places such as 'the Horseshoe', 'Death Valley', 'the Five Sisters', and 'the Five Brothers' became forever etched in the annals of the Marine Corps. Marine combat correspondent Sergeant W. F. Conway recalled that the 'Jap-infested' caves were 'dug at staggered levels through solid coral and limestone which ran through hundreds of yards of Peleliu's treacherous hills and ravines... Throughout the campaign hundreds and thousands of tons of explosives were thrown at the hills to level them and seal the caves'.

After a week of such fighting, during which they were hampered by typhoon rains, dysentery, and a shortage of rations, the 1st Marines were exhausted. With 56 per cent of their total, amounting to 1,749 men, either killed or wounded, the unit was incapable of further effective combat, and was replaced by the 7th Marines, who continued the deadly operation. As he limped aboard a ship bound for Pavuvu, one member of the 1st Marines growled: 'We're not a regiment, we're the *survivors* of a regiment.'

The situation was relieved with the arrival of the 321st Infantry on 23 September. In conjunction with elements of the 7th Marines, the GIs surrounded the Umurbrogol. After a further week of bitter fighting, a battalion commander of the 7th Marines reported: 'The men are very tired.' On 5 October, the 5th Marines took over from the 7th, which was by then a spent force. Eugene B. Sledge, 3rd Battalion, 5th Marines, and author of *With the Old Breed at Peleliu and Okinawa*, wrote: 'The struggle for survival went on day after day, night after night... time lost all meaning. A lull of hours or days seemed but a fleeting instant of heaven-sent tranquility. Lying in a foxhole sweating out an enemy artillery or mortar barrage or waiting to dash across open ground under machine gun or artillery fire defied any concept of time.'

The Landing on Tinian, in the Mariana Islands, took place on 24 July 1944. By nightfall of 'J-Day', all three infantry regiments of the 4th Marine Division, plus four pack howitzer battalions, were ashore at a cost of 15 killed and 225 wounded. At nightfall, the expected Japanese counterattack came, including tanks which rumbled towards the 23rd Marines through the shadowy light of US Navy star shells. Bracing themselves, the Marines opened fire with half-tracks,

anti-tank guns, and bazookas. An observer, First Lieutenant J. G. Lucas, recalled: 'The three lead tanks broke through our wall of fire. One began to glow blood-red, turned crazily on its tracks, and careened into a ditch. A second, mortally wounded, turned its machine guns on its tormentors, firing into the ditches in a last desperate effort to fight its way free. One hundred yards more it stopped dead in its tracks. The third tried frantically to turn and then retreat,

but our men closed in, literally blasting it apart. Bazookas knocked out the fourth tank with a direct hit which killed the driver. The rest of the crew piled out of the turret, screaming. The fifth tank, completely surrounded, attempted to flee. Bazookas made short work of it. Another hit set it afire, and its crew was cremated.' In the light of the burning wreckage, the Marines were able to see the closed ranks of the advancing Japanese infantry, and mowed them down.

The next morning, 1,241 enemy dead lay in and around the 4th Division's lines. According to divisional commander Major General Clifton B. Cates, this single, fierce action 'broke the Jap's back'! The plate depicts the moment after the fourth tank was knocked out by a two-man Marine bazooka team using an M1A1 rocket launcher. An anti-tank gun and crew is seen beyond them, with riflemen hugging the ground around. The Navy Corpsman in the foreground bears white stencilled discs

on his helmet cover and coat. These had been adopted for the Tarawa assault because the Geneva Convention Red Cross brassard offered an inviting target for Jap snipers. The Navajo radio operator on the right is sending messages in his own tongue, which the Japanese never managed to decipher! *Painting by Richard Hook*

With his unit fighting on for another 11 days, despite having already been in action for three weeks, Major F. O. Hough observed: 'Every Marine fighting in those hills is an expert. If he wasn't, he wouldn't be alive.' As a tribute of respect, the ship's crew of the USS *Mount McKinley* sent ashore its entire allowance of recreational beer for these experts.

By mid-October, Japanese resistance in the Umurbrogol had been severely reduced, and the work of the 1st Marine Division was done. Marine casualties on Pelelui amounted to 1,252 dead and 6,526 wounded. Although the last major pocket of enemy defence had been overcome by

Taken from aft on an Amtrac, this photo shows the view the Marines had of Mount Suribachi as they approached Iwo Jima on 19 February 1945.
Peter Newark's Military Pictures

the Army 81st Division by 25 November, it was not until 1955 that the last Japanese soldiers came out of the coral labyrinth and surrendered.

The reoccupation of the Philippines began on 20 October 1944, and 1,258 Marine artillerymen of V Amphibious Corps were among the first Americans to go ashore at Leyte. As they landed, someone stuck a sign on the beach which read: 'By the grace of God and a few Marines, MacArthur's back in the Philippines'! During the beach assault, the Japanese fleet hit the invasion force with everything it had, including the suicidal *kamikaze* planes. When the Battle of Leyte Gulf was over, the Japanese Imperial Navy largely ceased to exist.

UNCOMMON VALOR

The struggle for Iwo Jima, or 'Sulphur Island', which began on 19 February 1945, was the costliest battle in the history of the Marine Corps. Part of the Prefecture of Tokyo, and only 670 miles from the capital, Iwo was regarded by many as 'the gateway to Japan'. The capture of this 'bad-smelling pork chop of an island', seven and a half square miles in size, would provide an emergency landing site for the B-29s flying from Tinian to fire-bomb Tokyo. The radar stations on Iwo gave the home islands two hours warning of each approaching wave of raiders, and enabled Jap fighter planes to swarm up to meet the unescorted bombers. A 'thorn in the side' of the Army Airforce, Iwo Jima had to be taken, but the prize would not come easy. The fighting that took place during the 36-day assault would be immortalized in the words of Commander, Pacific Fleet/Commander in Chief, Pacific Ocean Areas, Admiral Chester W. Nimitz, who said, 'Among the Americans who served on Iwo Island, uncommon valor was a common virtue.'

In charge of the Japanese forces on Iwo Jima was Lieutenant General Tadamichi Kuribayashi, a cavalry officer, poet, and one-time commander of the Emperor's Imperial Guard, whose 'partly protruding belly', commented Radio Tokyo, was 'packed full of strong fighting spirit'. His garrison consisted of 23,000 well-armed, veteran infantry. Like the defenders of Peleliu, General Kuribayashi ordered his men to dig in, mixing cement with the coarse, black volcanic ash to form an impenetrable system of multi-storeyed, underground tunnels and defense works. In total, there were 730 major defense installations, containing 120 large calibre guns, 130 howitzers, 90 rocket launchers and mortars, 69 anti-tank guns, over 200 machine guns, and 24 tanks. At Iwo's southern tip was Mount Suribachi, a volcano which loomed 600 feet above the soft, terraced beaches. Farther north, the terrain rose into the Motoyama Plateau, where the Japanese had established two airfields and had another under construction.

Lessons had been learned since Tarawa. The US Navy had formed Underwater Demolition Teams to check beach and surf conditions, and to find and remove mines and other treacherous obstacles. On 17 February, rocket-firing boats slammed the beaches of Iwo to cover the approach of the Navy frogmen. Mistaking the LCI gunboats for the main US invasion force, the Japanese revealed their carefully concealed gun positions, and many were knocked out as they drew the fire of the US Navy. If they had remained undetected, these guns could have wreaked havoc on D-Day.

The assault on Iwo Jima began 48 hours later. Thunderous US naval shelling preceded it, but greatly disappointed the landing forces. The Marine commanders, Lieutenant General Holland Smith and Major General Harry Schmidt, had asked for a ten day preliminary bombardment, but got only three days. The Navy claimed it needed to conserve ammunition for the forthcoming invasion of Okinawa. The Marines also complained that they had been partially denied air cover, including eight Marine air squadrons, as carrier Task Force 58 was despatched to bomb Japan on 16 February. Admiral Spruance maintained that these carrier

attacks prevented Japan-based aircraft from interfering with the Iwo Jima landings. Whatever the reasons, the Marines lacked optimal gunfire preparation on 19 February.

The treacherous Iwo coastline afforded only two landing beaches worthy of the name, and both were in the southeast of the island. General Schmidt would land two Marine Divisions abreast— the 4th Division on the right, and the 5th on the left, next to Mount Suribachi.

General Holland Smith would hold the 3rd Division in reserve. Major General Clifton Cates had already taken the 4th Marine Division through the Marshalls and the Marianas. Major General Keller E. Rockey was new to the Pacific Campaign, and led the well-trained 5th Division into its first battle. Major General Graves B. Erskine commanded the 3rd Division, which contained the veterans of Bougainville and Guam.

At a conference on the eve of the assault, Secretary of the Navy James Forrestal

A pen and ink sketch of the landings on Iwo Jima, by Harry Reeks.
*Anne S.K. Brown
Military Collection*

commented: 'This next target, Iwo Jima, like Tarawa, leaves very little choice except to take it by force of arms, by character, and courage... My hat is off to the Marines.'

Of the moment the landing craft churned towards the island's blackened beaches that cool, breezy February morning, General Holland Smith recalled: 'Anyone who has been there can shut his eyes and see the place again. It never looked more aesthetically ugly than on D-day morning, or more completely Japanese. Its silhouette was like a sea monster, with the little dead volcano for the head, and the beach area for the neck, and all the rest of it, with its scrubby brown cliffs for the body. It had the minute, fussy compactness of those Japanese gardens. Its stones and rocks were like those contorted, wind-scoured, water-worn boulders which the Japanese like to collect as landscape decorations.'

The 8,000 assault troops hit the beaches precisely at H-hour, or 0902. The first threat was not the enemy, but the beach itself. The soft black sand made walking extremely difficult, and quickly immobilized all wheeled vehicles. An American journalist who accompanied the first assault wave recorded: 'The prevailing winds reversed themselves during the first ten days... so that the beachhead was exposed to the sullen fury of the

Pacific Ocean. Because Iwo Jima is a volcano rising straight out of the sea, there is no shallow water. The box-shaped landing craft were tossed about like egg-crates caught on the crest of a spring flood. Unprotected by breakwaters or coral reefs, the boats were swamped by six-foot breakers as soon as their bows rammed into the volcanic sand. The boats floundered, sank, and were spewn along the shore to form twisted barricades of debris.'

Minutes ticked by after the initial landings, and the Marines were met only by light small arms fire. Fleeting hopes of a 'cake walk' might have crossed the minds of some of the untried riflemen, but the veterans felt their skin begin to crawl. Fred E. Haynes, Regimental Operations Officer, 28th Marines, recalled: 'It was a very eerie landscape, I mean weird! Like a moon walk-about. You couldn't see the Japanese. I think all of us had this feeling too, where you just didn't know whether somebody had you in his sights!'

Having consulted their German allies after the Normandy landings of 6 June 1944, the Japanese had learned the wisdom of not contesting an overwhelming invasion force at the water's edge. Suddenly a series of flares bloomed overhead, and the expected fire-storm began. Kuribayashi had patiently waited until the beaches were clogged with men and vehicles, and when his gunners finally opened fire, they simply could not miss the 30,000 Marines packed into only two or three square miles of volcanic ash. According to Lieutenant Colonel 'Jumping Joe' Chambers, 3rd Battalion, 25th Marines: 'You could have held up a cigarette and lit it on the stuff going by!'

Landing on the left flank, the 28th Marines, commanded by Colonel H. Liversidge, had the task of cutting the island in two, and then surmounting Mount Suribachi. The 25th Marines, under Colonel J. R. Lanigan, landing on the right flank, would seize the dominating heights and then serve as a hinge for the entire force to strike north. General Cates knew the right flank would be hit by the most

A Japanese canteen, carried in an early-pattern US Marine Corps pouch, was captured at Iwo Jima. Both sides freely 'requisitioned' such equipage from the fallen foe. *Photo by the author, courtesy of Jim Moran*

severest fire, and prior to the assault had commented: 'If I knew the name of the man on the extreme right of the right-hand squad of the right-hand company of the 25th Marines, I'd recommend him for a medal before we go in.'

Ahead of the Marines, the fleet fired a ferocious 'rolling barrage' which slammed down steadily as they secured the beach area. As Fred E. Haynes recalled: 'Each regiment had a cruiser assigned to it, each battalion had a destroyer, and each division had a battleship. So we had an enormous amount of fire support available to us.'

Exposed to the most galling fire, and suffering dreadful casualties, the Marines began to creep forward in small groups. Members of B Company, 28th Marines reached the far shore across the island's neck in the first 90 minutes, thereby isolating Mount Suribachi from the rest of the island. Along the way, Captain Dwayne E. Mears, armed only with a pistol, attacked enemy machine gun nests until he was killed. Corporal Tony Stein, A Company, 28th Marines, used an improvised, hand-held machine gun, taken from a crashed Navy fighter's gun, to wipe out several pillboxes, thereby killing about 20 Japanese. He struggled back barefoot to the landing beach eight times for fresh ammunition, and on each occasion dragged back a wounded Marine. For his outstanding bravery, the 24 year old veteran of Guadalcanal and Bougainville received the Medal of Honor.

Meanwhile, other battalions of the 28th faced south in a futile attempt to scale Mount Suribachi. Armour was needed, but the first 16 Sherman tanks to come ashore could not get off the beach. According to plan, the 4th Division swung north but hit a storm of mortar fire, and the 15-foot sand terraces again stopped tanks and armoured amphibians. Without support, the riflemen of the 25th Regiment floundered in loose black sand.

Thus, about 30,000 Marines remained pinned down in a beachhead about 3,000 yards long and between 1,500 and 700 yards deep. Unlike Tarawa,

The front cover of the British edition of the US Army magazine *Yank*, dated 13 April 1945, featuring Marines on Iwo Jima. An observer pinpoints a Japanese machine gun nest on his map so that an artillery unit can eliminate it. *Peter Newark's Military Pictures*

there was not even a seawall to hide behind. A hardened veteran of previous campaigns, Sergeant T. Grady Gallant was appalled by the Marine body fragments and entrails which began to litter the ashes: 'The exact word that told all that was happening on this morning at this miserable place was carnage.' By nightfall, casualties amounted to almost 2,300 killed and wounded. Among the dead was Gunnery Sergeant John Basilone, 27th Marines, who, in 1942, had been awarded the Medal of Honor at Guadalcanal. A battler to the last, he had just cleaned out a blockhouse when a mortar blast cut him down.

With the enemy too disorganised to counterattack that night, the Marines took advantage of the respite afforded by darkness. Well short of the first day's objectives, most of them had yet to see a live Japanese, and not a single prisoner had been taken. Resolutely, they dug-in and secured their lines.

MOUNT SURIBACHI

The following day saw more positive progress with the capture of Motoyama Airfield No. 1, and the beginning of the assault on Mount Suribachi. A member of the 28th Marines recalled being involved for the next three days in 'a foot-by-foot crawl with mortars, artillery, rockets, machine guns, and grenades making us hug every rock and shell-hole. Rock slides were tumbled down on our heads by the Japs, and also as a result of our own naval gunfire… Each pill-box was a separate problem, an intricately designed fortress that had to be smashed into ruins… The walls of many began with 2-foot-thick concrete blocks, laced with iron rails. Then came ten to twelve feet of rocks, piled with dirt and the dirty ashes of Iwo…. Single entranceways, which were tiny, long holes, and one or two casemate openings were protected against direct hits or flying shrapnel by concrete abutments. The whole structure might look from the outside

like a mound rising a few feet above the surrounding ground.'

At 0800 hours on 23 February, a patrol of 40 men from 3rd Platoon, E Company, 2nd Battalion, 28th Marines, led by 1st Lieutenant Harold G. Schrier, assembled at the base of Mount Suribachi. The platoon's mission was to take the crater of Suribachi's peak and raise the U.S. flag. It was vital that 'Old Glory' should now be shown at the summit. Once achieved, it would be a blow to Japanese Imperial hopes, and a boost to the morale of the US Marines. The platoon slowly climbed the steep trails to the summit, but incredibly encountered no enemy fire. Reaching the top, the patrol members took positions around the crater watching for pockets of enemy resistance as others looked for something on which to raise the flag.

At 1020, the flag was hoisted on a steel pipe above the island by platoon commander Lieutenant Schrier, Platoon Sergeant Ernest I. Thomas, Jr., Sergeant Harry O. Hansen, Corporal Charles W. Lindberg, PFC James R. Michels, and Private Louis Charlo, a Crow Indian.

According to Regimental Operations Officer, Fred E. Haynes: 'The first flag was so small that you couldn't see it all the way up the island. The word was— "Get a bigger flag!" There's some confusion… as to who did what about that time, but Greeley Welles, who was the adjutant of the 2nd Battalion, sent a runner back to the beach, and apparently got the big flag off an LST. The second raising, coincidentally… happened when Joe Rosenthal was standing over to the side… and immediately snapped several pictures.'

Hence one of the most electrifying moments in US military history was captured forever by the camera lens as six more Marines raised the flag of Landing Ship Tank 779. This symbol of victory sent a wave of strength to the battle-weary fighting men below and in the fleet off the shore. A great cheer swept around the island. Ships ripped loose with their whistles and fog horns. For the first time in the

Many of the water colour paintings produced by Harry Reeks were considered too realistic for publication by the US government, and were eventually returned to the artist unused. The 'thousand-yard stare' is clearly evident on this exhausted Marine's face.
Anne S.K. Brown Military Collection

long war, an American flag had been raised over Japanese home territory. But the struggle was not yet over, and the 28th Marines, assisted by the 5th Engineer Battalion, set about destroying 165 concrete pillboxes and sealing the 200 Jap-infested caves that remained within the bowels of the volcano.

The 3rd Marine Division, joined the fighting on the fifth day of the battle. These Marines immediately began the mission of securing Airfield No. 2 in the centre sector of the island. Each division fought hard to gain ground against a determined Japanese defender. The Japanese leaders knew with the fall of Suribachi and the capture of the airfields that the Marine advance on the island could not be stopped. But they would make the Marines fight for every inch of land they won.

A proud moment for those who worked so hard to gain control of the island was when the first emergency landing was made by a B-29 bomber on 4 March. Repairs were made, refueling was completed and the aircraft was off to complete its mission.

Meanwhile, General Kuribayashi concentrated his energies and his forces in the central and northern sections of the island. Miles of interlocking caves, concrete blockhouses and pillboxes proved to be one of the most impenetrable defenses encountered by the Marines in the Pacific.

As the Marine divisions advanced north, three abreast, General Schmidt brought in the 55mm howitzers to beef up fire support. The 3rd Marine Division encountered the main Japanese defence line in their move to take Airfield No. 2. Ringed with hundreds of pillboxes, the enemy artillery was sited to fire straight along the open runways. As with most of the fighting on Iwo Jima, frontal assault was the method used to gain every inch of ground, and finally, after dreadful casualties, the riflemen of the 21st Marines, led by Lieutenant Dominick J. Grossi, reached the ridge beyond the airfield. Ankle-deep in sand, they fought with rifle butts, bayonets, and knives, and opened up a gap in the Japanese defences.

Despite this success, the Marines got bogged down in the face of further stubborn Japanese resistance. In desperation, General Erskine changed tactics and, during the early hours of 7 March, ordered one of the few Marine battalion-size night attacks of the Pacific War. The 21st Marines, and the 3rd Battalion, 9th Marines, did indeed surprise the enemy but as dawn broke, found they had captured the wrong hill. Their real objective, Hill 362C, was still 250 yards further to their front. Regardless of having lost the element of surprise, they continued their operation, and in a vicious fire-fight finally captured their real objective. The Marines now held much of the high ground on the Motoyama Plateau, and, reaching the northeastern coast by 9 March, had effectively cut the island lengthwise in two. To prove it, the patrol leader who first reached the coast, filled a canteen

This study by Harry Reeks reveals the horror of Iwo Jima in stark reality. Shell-torn American bodies litter the landing area.
Anne S.K. Brown Military Collection

with sea-water and sent it back to General Erskine labelled, 'For inspection, not consumption'!

But the campaign continued to take its toll, and by the end of the second week of fighting, the Marines were decimated, with casualties amounting to 16,000! One man recalled bitterly: 'They send you up to a place... and you get shot to hell and maybe they pull you back. But then they send you right up again and then you get murdered. God, you stay there until you get killed or until you can't stand it anymore.'

First Lieutenant J. G. Lucas, 23rd Marines, recorded: 'It takes courage to stay at the front on Iwo Jima. It takes something which we can't tag or classify to push out ahead of those lines, against an unseen enemy who has survived two months of shell and shock, who lives beneath the rocks of the island, an enemy capable of suddenly appearing on your flanks or even at your rear, and of disappearing back into his hole. It takes courage for officers to send their men ahead, when many they've known since the Division came into existence have already gone. It takes courage to crawl ahead 100 yards a day, and get up the next morning, count losses, and do it again. But that's the only way it can be done.'

On the left of the 3rd Marine Division, the 5th Marine Division pushed up the western coast from the central airfield to the island's northern tip. Moving to seize and hold the eastern portion of the island, the 4th Marine Division encountered a mini-*banzai* charge, as surviving members of the Japanese Navy on Iwo disobeyed Kuribayashi's orders and launched a night attack. This action effectively shortened the campaign for the Marines, who found almost 700 Japanese dead in front of their lines the next morning.

Operations entered the final phases on 11 March, as enemy opposition became less centralised, and individual pockets of resistance were taken one by one. According to Captain Frank C. Caldwell, whose men had just captured a pillbox using flame-throwers: 'Out came a smouldering Japanese and held up a cocked grenade. He was getting ready to throw, in spite of the fact he couldn't see... My men dropped him right there. We went over to inspect him and see if we could find any information on the man. We lifted his helmet off his head and low and behold we found a little photograph... and there was a picture of this Japanese with his family, all standing at attention. And even the most hardened Marine I had there choked up when he saw that!'

Finally on 26 March, following a further *banzai* attack against troops and air corps personnel near the beaches, the island was declared secure. The US Army's 147th Infantry Regiment assumed ground control of the island on 4 April, thereby relieving the largest body of Marines committed in combat in one operation during World War II.

The 36-day assault resulted in more than 26,000 American casualties, including 6,800 dead. Of the 20,000 Japanese defenders, only 1,083 survived. The Marines' efforts, however, provided a vital link in the US chain of bomber bases. By the war's end, 2,400 B-29 bombers carrying 27,000 crewmen made unscheduled landings on Iwo Jima. Twenty-seven Medals of Honor were awarded to Marines and sailors. Many more were awarded posthumously than for any other single operation during the war.

OKINAWA

One more island lay ahead, and it would be the scene of the largest battle of the Pacific War. By late October 1944, Okinawa, in the Ryukyu Island chain, had been targeted for invasion by Allied forces. Located strategically between Kyushu, the southernmost island of Japan, and Formosa, today called Taiwan, Okinawa was viewed as the base from which assault troops could stage and train for the attack on the Japanese mainland. The island had several airfields and the only two substantial harbours between Formosa and Kyushu. It was also defended by the 32nd Army, estimated at 110,000 men, under the command of Lieutenant General Mitsuru Ushijima, one of the most capable officers in the Japanese Imperial forces.

The greatest armada ever was assembled for 'Operation Iceberg'. Admiral Spruance's 5th fleet included more than 40 aircraft carriers, 18 battleships, 200 destroyers and hundreds of assorted support ships. The assault force consisted of 182,00 troops of the US 10th Army, of which 81,000 were Marines. The four principal commanders were Admiral Spruance, Vice Admiral Marc Mitscher, leading Task Force 58, Vice Admiral Richmond Kelly Turner, Task Force 51, and Lieutenant General Simon Bolivar Buckner, grandson of the Confederate general of the same name, commanding the US 10th Army. Their battle plan envisioned a week of preliminary air strikes from the fast carriers and by B-29s from the Marianas Islands, followed by eight days of naval bombardment preceding the landings.

The invasion force was composed of Major General Roy S. Geiger's 3rd Amphibious Corps with its three Marine divisions, the 1st, 2nd and 6th, and four infantry divisions of the 24th Army Corps. The 2nd Marine Division would stage a feint landing on the southern end of the island, while the real attack force rushed ashore on the west coast, thereby

cutting the defenders in two. These landings would take place over five miles of beaches on the west coast of southern Okinawa. Known as the 'Hagushi beaches', they were named after a village which was actually called Tosuchi, at the mouth of the Bishigawa River. The river was the boundary between the Marines' sector in the north and the Army's in the south. The location was chosen for its close proximity to the Yontan and Kadena airfields, which needed to be captured quickly to help land-based planes fend off enemy air attacks. These forces would then spread out east and south to capture other territory. Northern Okinawa, the Motobu Peninsula, and nearby Ie Shima island and airfield would be captured later.

Japanese forces at Okinawa hoped to delay the final assault on Japan. Having lost most forward air bases and aircraft carriers, the Japanese high command planned once again to emphasize *kamikaze*, suicide-piloted aircraft attacks on Allied ships. A massed air attack by both *kamikazes* and conventional aircraft was planned as part of the defense.

PFC Weldon Townsend, 3rd Battalion, 2nd Marines, was aboard one of the LSTs involved in the diversionary attack conducted by the 2nd Division, and recalled: 'We were heading for the Chinen Peninsula to make the early morning feint,

In this magnificent view of Mount Suribachi, Harry Reeks catches the moment a Sherman tank is brought up to assist the Marines huddled in a foxhole in the foreground. The whole eerie scene is lit by star shells and exploding shells.
Anne S.K. Brown Military Collection

April Fool Day, 1945. At approximately 0600 the Japanese Suicide Plane hit I Company's LST, setting it on fire. I had just gone on deck of my LST because I couldn't sleep and I felt safer outside, when I witnessed the hit. The plane's engines ripped through the LST and exploded in the Amtrak compartment, killing and wounding the sleeping marines in the Amtraks... I'll never forget that day or the Kamikaze days that followed. My LST had at least two or three near misses during the attacks. I truly believe that there is nothing more terrifying than having a man, Hellbent on committing suicide, guiding his winged bomber at you. I had been through the banzai attacks but, we were able to control those. We had no control over the Divine Wind of the Japanese.'

Meanwhile, US forces offshore on the west coast of the island of Okinawa had no inkling that the beaches had been left intentionally undefended and that the Japanese troops were dug in, occupying caves, cement tombs, and fortifications, all of which were well protected from the pre-invasion bombardment.

After Naval Underwater Demolition Teams had reconnoitered the Hagushi beaches on Good Friday, 30 March, the amphibious assault on Okinawa began at 0830 hours on 1 April. By 0400, the beachhead was secured. Over 50,000 troops had been put ashore and were ready to advance, Marines to the north and west and GIs to the south. The question was, 'Where were the Japanese?' Eugene B. Sledge, 5th Marines, recalled: 'There was no opposition. Nobody was fired at. We just couldn't believe it. It was the first good news we had during the war, and everybody started singing 'Little Brown Jug'. But we knew they were up to something, as they weren't gonna give that island up cheap.'

American intelligence had seriously underestimated Japanese strength on the island. As a result, the 2nd Marine Division was unwisely shipped back to Saipan without ever setting foot on Okinawa. But as the Marines of the 1st and 6th Divisions advanced inland, their worst fears began to be confirmed. The day after landing, the 22nd Marines walked into a deep ravine and the whole hillside erupted with enemy gunfire, killing all but ten of Lieutenant Daniel Brewster's platoon before reinforcements arrived. The slogging match had begun.

BATTLE FATIGUE

By 8 April, the US forces were stopped cold at the first Japanese defense line by pillboxes with steel doors impervious to flame-throwers! Casualties were heavy. Reinforcements were landed on 9 April, and American troops ashore now numbered 160,000.

Japanese forces were concentrated in the Mobotu Peninsula, northwest of the invasion beaches, and it took the 6th Marine Division until 20 April to wipe them out. Meanwhile, in the south of the island, attention focussed on the capture of Shuri Castle, an ancient fortification and the key defensive position for Japanese resistance, underneath which was General Ushijima's command post. The castle was located on a high point midway between the eastern and western beaches. Its strongly prepared defensive positions with interlocking fields of fire and interconnected tunnels proved extremely difficult and costly to overrun. As the fighting dragged on, battle fatigue began to take its toll among the Marines.

Serving on the 'Shuri Line', Eugene Sledge, 5th Marines, recalled: 'We ran forward into these positions, and they were firing at us at least one 8-inch gun that was blowing trees out of the ground! They were battery firing 150 mm howitzers and 75 mm guns. And it was just one eruption of explosions after another in that concentrated area... How many soldiers I saw get killed as they tried to move out! Some of them got into shell holes and wouldn't move! They had to practically drag them out to get them to the rear!'

The late spring rains made combat conditions even more intolerable during this part of the campaign. William Manchester, 29th Marines, who served two months in the line, recalled: '...most of the time... You were fully exposed to it, and helpless in deluges. By the time you had a hole dug, a couple of inches of rain had already gathered in it. Tossing shrubs in didn't help; their branches jabbed you. You wrapped yourself in your poncho or shelter half, but the water always seeped through. You lapsed into a coma of exhaustion and wakened in a drippy, misty dawn with your head fuzzy and a terrible taste in your mouth resembling... "a Greek wrestler's jockstrap".'

Eugene Sledge endured the most appalling conditions below Sugar Loaf Hill: 'When enemy artillery shells exploded in the area, the eruptions of soil and mud uncovered previously buried Japanese dead and scattered chunks of corpses. Like the area around our gun pits, the ridge was a stinking compost pile. If a Marine slipped and slid down the back slope of the muddy ridge, he was apt to reach the bottom vomiting. I saw more than one man lose his footing and slip and slide all the way to the bottom only to stand up horror-stricken as he watched in disbelief while fat maggots tumbled out of his muddy dungaree pockets, cartridge belt, legging lacings, and the like. Then he and a buddy would shake or scrape them away with a piece of ammo box or knife blade.'

The Japanese defense line was finally broken on 28 April. Attacking the two flanks of the Japanese forces, Buckner's troops fought fiercely against the enemy. By 21 May, the Japanese had withdrawn to the southern tip of the island. The 10th Army occupied the capital, Naha, on 27 May. Two days later, Japanese troops began withdrawing from Shuri, shortly after which A Company, 1st Battalion, 5th Marines captured the remains of Shuri Castle, and raised the flag of the 1st Division over Ushijima's last stronghold.

In driving rain on 4 June 1945, the 4th Marines,

followed by the 29th Marines, conducted the last amphibious assault of the Second World War. Landing on the Oroku Peninsula, southeast of Naha, they broke the Sugar Loaf deadlock, compressing the remaining Japanese into a corner, and then into oblivion. More than 4,000 of the enemy died in the space of ten days, at a cost of 1,608 Marines killed and wounded.

Meanwhile General Buckner's 10th Army moved on the enemy's position at Mabuni, an escarpment located on the southern tip of the island. Its natural and man-made caves proved nearly impenetrable for any but Buckner's 'blow torch and corkscrew' method of fighting, employing flame-throwers and high explosives to force a way into the enemy's defensive positions. In the end, it took hand-to-hand combat, aerial bombardment and tanks with flame-throwers to capture the entrenched and fiercely defiant Japanese troops.

Tragically, General Buckner was hit and killed by a coral fragment thrown up by Japanese artillery shell fire on 18 June. Marine General Roy Geiger assumed temporary command of 10th Army until relieved five days later by Army General Joseph A. Stilwell. On 19 June, the Japanese commander ordered all remaining defenders to fight to the death. On the 21st, the 10th Army pushed through to the southernmost point on Okinawa. Ushijimi and his chief of staff committed *hara kiri* rather than accept defeat. Geiger announced the island secured and a formal flag-raising ceremony took place on 22 June. The 82-day Okinawan campaign was officially declared over on 2 July 1945.

Total American casualties on Okinawa exceeded 68,000, of which 20,020 were Marines plus attached Navy corpsmen. Of the latter figure, 3,561 were battle deaths. The Marines were still on Okinawa getting ready for the invasion of Japan when the atom bombs were dropped on Hiroshima and Nagasaki, thereby ending the war. When the Japanese surrendered aboard the battleship *Missouri* on 2 September 1945,

the only senior Marine officer present was Roy Geiger, commander of the Fleet Marine Force, Pacific. Three days earlier, some of the first American forces to set foot on Japanese home soil since the beginning of the war were the 2nd Battalion, 4th Marines — a regiment reborn after its surrender at Corregidor back in May 1942.

At the end of the Second World War, there were 458,000 men and women, divided into six divisions, and six air wings, serving in the US Marine Corps. The Marine casualty list for the Pacific campaign consisted of 19,733 killed in action, 67,207 wounded, 348 prisoners of war, and 4,778 other deaths. Out of a total of 433 Medals of Honor awarded to American servicemen during the entire conflict, 80 were received by the Marines, of which 50 were awarded posthumously.

Ernie Pyle, the much-loved US war correspondent, who was killed on 18 April during the Okinawa campaign, left the most moving tribute to the Marine Corps during the Pacific War: 'In peacetime, when the Marine Corps was a small outfit, with its campaigns high-lighted, everybody was a volunteer and you could understand why they felt so superior. But with the war the Marine Corps had grown by hundreds of thousands of men. It became an outfit of ordinary people— some big, some little, some even draftees. It had changed, in fact, until marines looked to me exactly like a company of soldiers in Europe. Yet the Marine Corps spirit still remained. I never did find out what perpetuated it. The men were not necessarily better trained, nor were they any better equipped; often they were not so well supplied as other troops. But the marine still considered himself a better soldier than anybody else, even though nine-tenths of them didn't want to be soldiers at all… No, marines don't thirst for battles. I've read and heard enough about them to have no doubts whatever about the things they can do when they have to. They are o.k. for my money, in battle or out.'

Private Conrad, 1st Marine Division, inspects a piece of shrapnel which narrowly missed him in his foxhole on Okinawa, 1945. Note the spare magazine pouch on the butt-stock of his M1 carbine.
NA 127-N-126654

A Marine attempts to comfort a battle-weary comrade who broke down and cried after seeing one of his close friends die fighting the Japanese on the 'Shuri Line' on Okinawa, main island in the Ryukyu chain.
Imperial War Museum Photo # NYF 80378

THE MARINE LEGACY

During the half century following the Second World War, the US Marine Corps has continued to earn its reputation as one of the world's elite military organisations. Serving in Korea, Vietnam, Lebanon, the Gulf War and, most recently, in the Balkans conflict, the Marines have faced a variety of enemies and adversities.

As a wave of euphoria swept across America following the surrender of Japan in 1945, and other branches of the US armed forces returned home for demobilization, the Marines stayed put in the Far East, occupying North China to prevent Manchuria from falling into Russian Communist hands. No invasion came, although numerous clashes with the Chinese Communists kept the men of the 1st and 6th Marine Divisions, supported by the 1st Marine Air Group, very busy. Eventually, public pressure in the US to 'Bring the boys home' led to the Marine presence in China being halved by mid-1946. Meanwhile, before the end of 1945, Congress had set the peacetime strength of the Marine Corps at 107,000, nearly six times its pre-war size but under a quarter of its peak wartime strength of 484,631.

With victory over the Chinese Nationalists in sight for Mao Zedong, the Marines helped evacuate Americans from Shanghai during December 1948, and the last 'Leathernecks' left China six months later. The establishment of Red China was to have a profound effect on future US affairs in the Far East, and the huge Red Army would soon provide the Marines with their next major test of arms.

At dawn on 25 June 1950, the North Korean People's Army (NKPA) crossed the 38th Parallel and invaded South Korea, catching the free world off guard. The United Nations Security Council, with the Soviet delegate voluntarily absent, invoked military sanctions against North Korea two days later. Commandant Clifton Cates offered immediate Marine support to General Douglas MacArthur, commander of the UN forces destined for Korea. As a result, the 1st Provisional Marine Brigade landed at Pusan, and the 5th Marines went into

action accompanied by close air support from MAG-1's Corsairs on 7 August 1950 – the 8th anniversary of Guadalcanal.

Six days later, during the battle of the 'Naktong Bulge', the 5th Marines were ordered to take 'No-Name Ridge', where they clashed for the first time with the much vaunted Russian-built T-34 tanks. The 9th NKPA Division soon fell back in disorder as battle-hardened veterans of the Pacific War tore into them with rocket launchers, recoilless rifles, and 90 mm tank fire. Meanwhile back in the US, President Truman reactivated the Organised Marine Corps Reserve, and a further 33,528 veterans found themselves on the way to Korea as part of the reconstructed 1st Marine Division.

The North Koreans thought an amphibious assault on Inchon, midway along the west coast of the Korean peninsula, was impossible. So did the Pentagon when General MacArthur outlined his plan! Nonetheless, on 15 September 1950, the US X Corps including the 1st Marine Division, plus 3,000 South Korean Marines, commanded by General Holland Smith, scrambled ashore there despite difficult tides, no beach, and high sea walls. By the end of the day, a substantial foothold had been secured, and MacArthur was able to radio the fleet: 'The Navy and the Marines have never shone so brightly than this morning.' By 27 September, the hard-fighting UN forces had cut the North Korean supply lines, thereby isolating NKPA troops in the south, and relieving Seoul, the South Korean capital.

Believing North Korea was close to defeat, MacArthur next gained UN authorisation to send troops across the 38th Parallel to 'mop up' remaining pockets of NKPA opposition. As the 1st Marine Division marched north from Wonsan, he ignored reports that Red Chinese troops were massing near the Yalu River. In late October, a division of the Red Army crossed the Yalu and clashed with the 7th Marines near Sudong-ni. Unperturbed, MacArthur ordered an all-out two-

pronged attack north in order to 'end the war by Christmas'.

On 24 November, the hammer-blow struck as 100,000 Chinese troops swarmed into North Korea and fell upon the UN forces. Outnumbered and ill-equipped to face a fresh enemy, 40,000 US troops, including the 1st Marine Division, were cut off in a bitter North Korean winter. When asked by the press if he intended to retreat, General Smith is quoted as saying, 'Retreat hell! We're just attacking in another direction!'

With the assistance of Marine close air support, US ground forces came out fighting. Smashing their way repeatedly through the encircling enemy, they fought their way across the ice-bound ridges and through the deep winding valleys until, after 13 tortuous days, they reached the waiting ships in the harbour at Hungham. Regarding it as a 'march to glory', *Time* magazine concluded it was 'A battle unparalled in US military history. It had some of the aspects of Bataan, some of Anzio, some of Dunkirk, some of Valley Forge.' From the military perspective, the main tactical achievement of the withdrawal was that the 1st Marine Division had 'come through with all operable equipment, with wounded properly evacuated, and with tactical integrity'.

For the next two years, the fighting in Korea seesawed back and forth across the 38th Parallel

Top, **cloth patch worn by the 2nd Battalion, 9th Marines. This unit conducted one of the most successful regimental-sized actions of the Vietnam War. After a two-month campaign they cleared the A Shau/Da Krong valleys of Viet Cong.** *Peter Newark's Military Pictures*

Above, **a Marine armed with M16 rifle during the Vietnam War in 1968.** *Peter Newark's Military Pictures*

with neither side gaining the initiative. During this period the Marines spent much of their time in 'the alien occupation of land mass warfare' as part of Lieutenant General Matthew B. Ridgeway's 8th US Army. During January 1951 they began the 'Rice Paddy Patrols', searching out North Korean guerrillas in the South. Within a month, they had eliminated about 60 per cent of the enemy, whilst driving remaining units out of the area. Next spearheading 'Operation Ripper', the Marines led the offensive on the east central front, and by 4 April were among the first UN forces to re-cross the 38th Parallel where they subsequently stopped a major Chinese counter-offensive.

An eventual cease-fire was agreed at Panmunjon on 27 July 1953. The war in Korea had lasted three years, one month, and two days, and had proved a costly affair for the US. Total American casualties amounted to approximately 136,000 men killed, missing, or wounded, of which 28,011 were Marines. Earlier, on 25 March of that year, the 1st Marine Division had paraded behind the lines to receive the Korean Presidential Unit Citation, an award they still wear with pride to this day.

The Marine Corps emerged from the Korean War with the highest peacetime strength in its history. The suddenness of the war had emphasized the importance of maintaining the service as a ready strike force and, as a result of the 'Marine Corps Bill' of 1952, the 2nd and 3rd Divisions were re-activated with the latter being sent to Japan, while the former was held in reserve in the States.

During the remainder of the 1950s and early 1960s the US Marines travelled throughout the world, standing ready for immediate service whenever needed, and deploying where necessary. They were actively involved in the withdrawal of Chinese Nationalists to Formosa in 1955. The following year saw them back in Alexandria, Egypt, manning an evacuation centre during the Suez Crisis. In 1958, they were landed at Beirut when revolt threatened the stability of Lebanon after the

coup d'état and assassination of pro-Western King Faisal of nearby Iraq. When Fidel Castro seized control of Cuba during the same year, the Marines based at Guantanamo Bay were deployed to protect their water supply. Although they had no part to play in the disastrous Bay of Pigs landings, the entire Corps was put on red alert during the Cuban Missile Crisis of 1962.

Then there were the humanitarian missions. Marines assisted rescue victims of earthquakes in Turkey, Greece, and Morocco; flood victims were helped in Mexico, Spain, and Ceylon; and hurricane survivors in British Honduras.

VIETNAM

United States military assistance to South Vietnam dates back to 1954, when the US Military Assistance Advisory Group began to train the South Vietnamese Army to counter the communist threat from North Vietnam. During the same year the first Marine, Colonel Victor J. Croizat, joined that group as a liaison officer, and the Marines were committed to the next major conflict of the Cold War. Drill instructors began training South Vietnamese Marines, and by 1962 Medium Helicopter Squadron 362 had arrived to support Vietnamese forces, bringing the number of US Marines in Vietnam to 600. The escalation of the

A Bell AH-1 HueyCobra gunship of the Marine Corps. The HueyCobra entered US military service in 1966 and first saw service in Vietnam in mid-1967 as the AH-1G. *Peter Newark's Military Pictures*

war began for the Corps on 8 March 1965 when the 9th Marine Expeditionary Brigade (MEB) was sent to protect the US Air Force base at Da Nang from further Viet Cong raids. Marine strength at Da Nang quickly built to 5,000, although initially they were under orders to fire only if fired upon.

This purely defensive role became more difficult to maintain as four regiments of North Vietnamese regulars began to operate in the area, ambushing an Army of the Republic of Vietnam (ARVN) battalion. When Commandant Wallace Greene Jr. conducted an inspection tour of Vietnam in 1965, he insisted that his Marines were not there to 'sit on their ditty boxes, they were there to kill Viet Cong'. With the situation deteriorating rapidly, President Lyndon Baines Johnson ordered 125,000 US troops, including four Marine regiments and four Marine aircraft groups, to Vietnam.

Regimental Landing Team (RLT) 7, composed of the 7th Marines, the vanguard of the 1st Marine Division, began 'Operation Starlite' on 18 August 1965. In their first regimental-size action since the Korean War, the Marines struck at the 1st Viet Cong Regiment on the Van Tuong peninsula. The attack used both amphibious and helicopter-borne assault, and severely mauled the enemy, killing 964 VCs and forcing the remainder away from the coast. Henceforth, the Viet Cong would avoid stand-up battles with US forces and the guerilla tactics of the Vietnam War had arrived.

In 1966 the size of the Marine Corps in Vietnam continued to grow as the remainder of the 1st Marine Division, commanded by Major General Lewis J. 'Jeff' Fields, followed by the 3rd Marine Division, arrived to assist in the 'search and destroy' campaign. During the next eighteen months, the Marines fought 11 major operations of battalion size or larger, and mounted over 356,000 smaller unit patrols. Although nearly 18,000 enemy were killed, the cost to the Corps was high, with about 1,700 killed and over 9,000 wounded. Included in the former was the 3rd Division commander, Major General Bruno A. Hochmuth. And all with little real gain as North Vietnamese troops continued to pour quietly south along the 'Ho Chi Minh' trail.

Thus far in the conflict, a truce had been customary at Tet, the Vietnamese celebration of the lunar new year. In 1968 the Viet Cong broke the truce and, on 29 January, launched an all-out offensive which lasted 71 days, during which they attacked 105 cities and towns throughout South Vietnam. In particular, they captured the ancient city of Hue, once the capital of Indochina, and even briefly infiltrated Saigon, occupying the American embassy. The US counterattack involved three Marine and 13 ARVN battalions. After 26 days of house-to-house combat they had recaptured Hue City.

While Tet raged, another drama unfolded at Khe Sanh. For 77 days the 26th Marines, commanded by Colonel David E. Lownds, held the embattled base against intense pressure by the Viet Cong, who hurled as many as 1,000 shells a day into the Marine position. President Johnson became so concerned over the siege that he had an exact model of the Khe Sanh base built to monitor the situation on the ground. But Marine tenacity and American air power inflicted grievous losses upon the enemy. On 6 April, the Army's 1st Cavalry Division finally broke the siege.

The ferocity of the Tet Offensive, brought instantly to the TV screen, shocked the American public and convinced many that US forces should be withdrawn from Vietnam. As a growing number of American conscripts burned their draft cards to chants of 'Hell no! We won't go!', the US started to pull out of the Vietnam War. President Richard Nixon replaced LBJ and peace talks in Paris began to raise hopes for an end to the conflict.

But the war dragged on. In 1969, Colonel Robert H. Barrow's 9th Marines began 'Operation Dewey Canyon', perhaps the most successful high-mobility regimental-sized action of the war. For two months the Marines operated in the A Shau/Da Krong valleys. By 18 March, the Viet Cong base area had been cleared out, killing more than 1,600 enemy. The Marine air-ground team proved its worth in greatly reducing enemy 122 mm rocket fire into Da Nang. Marine infantry, transported by helicopters, cleared out enemy positions in the rugged 'Happy Valley' and 'Charlie Ridge' areas, all supported by effective Marine fixed-wing aircraft.

Meanwhile, American troops continued to be withdrawn, as Nixon's plan to 'Vietnamize' the war unfolded. Out of a total of 80,000 Marines in Vietnam at the beginning of 1969, only 55,000 remained by the year's end. Although large scale US offensives were over, it was not until 27 January 1973 that a peace treaty was finally signed in Paris. The last 'Leathernecks', consisting of the 3rd Marine Amphibious Brigade, had already flown out from Da Nang on 14 April 1971.

With the final collapse of South Vietnam in the Spring of 1975, the 9th Marine Amphibious Brigade mounted 'Operation Frequent Wind', during which they assisted in the rescue of nearly 5,000 American and Vietnamese civilians, who were helicoptered from the roof of the US Embassy in Saigon. A few weeks earlier, Marines had hauled down the flag over the US Embassy in Phnom Penh, capital of neighbouring Cambodia, and were on the last helicopter to fly out. The number of casualties sustained during the conflict in South-East Asia is a testimonial to the contribution made by the Marines. Between 1961 and 1975 the Corps lost a total of 12,983 killed and 88,591 wounded—nearly a third of all American casualties during the war.

WORLD CRISES

Even before the dust had settled on Vietnam, the Marines were involved in other world crises. In 1973, the Marine Amphibious Brigade of the 6th Fleet stood by in the Mediterranean when Egypt and Syria attacked Israel in what became known as the Yom Kippur War. The same force evacuated American citizens from Cyprus the following year when Archbishop Makarios was overthrown and Turkish troops landed on the island. After the Ayatollah Khomeini seized power in Iran in 1979, a mob stormed the US Embassy in Teheran, capturing 63 Americans, including the 13-man Marine detachment. Most of the hostages were held captive for 444 days before final release. During an abortive attempt to set them free on 24 April 1980, eight US servicemen, including three Marines, were killed when a helicopter collided with a KC-130 Hercules in the desert.

A bigger tragedy struck on 23 October 1983. While undertaking a peace-keeping mission in Lebanon after the Israelis had pulled their troops out of West Beirut, 220 Marines died when a truck crammed with an estimated six tons of explosives blew up. Another 40 Marines were to die before UN forces were finally withdrawn in February 1984. Meanwhile in the Caribbean, four hundred Marines were involved in a joint US operation to restore order and evacuate American citizens from Grenada between 25 October and 2 November, 1983. As the decade of the 1980s came to a close, Marines were summoned to respond to instability in Central America. 'Operation Just Cause' was conducted in Panama from 20 December 1989 until 31 January 1990 to overthrow the corrupt regime of Manuel Noriega, and restore the democratic process in that state.

Less than a year later, in August 1990, the Iraqi invasion of Kuwait set in motion events that would lead to the largest deployment of Marines since the Second World War. Between August 1990 and January 1991 some 24 infantry battalions and 40 air squadrons, totalling more than 92,000 Marines, were sent to the Persian Gulf as part of 'Operation Desert Shield'.

On 17 January 1991, the air campaign of 'Operation Desert Storm' began. The main attack came overland, beginning on 24 February when the 1st and 2nd Marine Divisions breached the

An élite force for all seasons. US Marine Corps field uniforms, circa 1983. *Peter Newark's Military Pictures*

US Marine Honor Guard
in dress blues.
United States Naval
Institute

Iraqi defense lines and stormed into occupied Kuwait. Meanwhile, the threat from the sea in the form of two Marine expeditionary brigades held in check some 50,000 Iraqis along the Kuwait coast. By the morning of 28 February, four days after the ground war began, almost the entire Iraqi Army in the Kuwaiti theatre of operations had been encircled with 4,000 tanks smashed and 42 divisions destroyed or rendered ineffective. Total US Marine losses during this short war amounted to 24 dead and 88 wounded in action.

Since the Gulf War, the Marine Corps has been involved in additional actions to counter Iraqi aggression. In October 1994, 'Operation Vigilant Warrior' saw the rapid deployment of US forces in Kuwait and Saudi Arabia to counter Iraqi military buildup south of the 32nd parallel. From August 1995, a Marine presence has remained in the Gulf area.

During the Balkans crisis in 1995, USAF pilot Captain Scott O'Grady was shot down while enforcing a no-fly zone over Bosnia-Hercegovina. On 8 June, the 24th Marine Expeditionary Unit, commanded by Colonel James L. Jones, conducted a successful 'tactical recovery of aircraft and personnel' (TRAP) mission, and rescued the beleaguered flyer during a daring daylight raid. During the following August and September, the 2nd Marine Air Wing conducted highly effective air strikes into Bosnia in support of UN resolutions as part of 'Operation Deliberate Force'.

The Corps has also been involved in numerous humanitarian operations around the world during recent years. Seven times since 1990, Marines have been called upon to evacuate civilians threatened by anarchy and civil strife in their country. In the aftermath of the Gulf War, when Baghdad began a campaign to suppress the dissident Kurdish minority in northern Iraq, over 3,600 Marines took part in 'Operation Provide Comfort', a three-month operation that successfully established a safe haven for the Kurds and staved off a humanitarian disaster.

One of the largest post-Cold War humanitarian operations began on 9 December 1992, when Marines landed in Somalia, beginning 'Operation Restore Hope'. Famine, caused by political chaos, threatened the lives of thousands of Somalis and the mission of the Marines was to secure major air and sea ports, key installations and food distribution points in order to permit the free passage of relief supplies threatened by a multitude of armed warlords.

The modern Marine Corps consists of 174,000 active duty Marines, 42,000 reservists, and about 18,000 supporting civilians. Of the former, 108,500 are in the Fleet Marine Force, of which 24,130 are 'forward deployed' as part of a flexible, multi-service strike force ready to go into action at a moment's notice. Marines can be sealifted or airlifted anywhere in the world. Once on station, they can be supported and sustained by Maritime Prepositioning Ships (MPS) until either the situation is under control, or reinforcements have arrived. Disaster and humanitarian assistance, counter-drug operations, noncombatant emergency evacuations, support for civil authority, all are familiar terms to Fleet Marine Force personnel over the past decade.

Indeed, the modern Marine stands ready to continue in the proud tradition of those who so valiantly fought and died at Bull Run, Belleau Wood, Tarawa, and Khe Sanh. As stated by General Charles C. Krulak, the 31st Commandant of the Marine Corps: 'Our warfighting legacy is one of duty, strength, sacrifice, discipline, and determination. These themes are cornerstones of the individual Marine and of our Corps... However, while we reflect on our past, let us also re-dedicate ourselves to a future of improvement. For, as good as we are now, we must be better tomorrow. The challenges of today are the opportunities of the 21st century. Both will demand much of us all.'

Next page, **the 4th Marine Expeditionary Brigade disembark from a 'Landing Craft, Medium', or LCM-6, while conducting amphibious assaults on Onslow Beach, North Carolina, during Tactical Commander's Amphibious Training exercises on 27 July 1988.** *United States Naval Institute*

Military Illustrated is the leading monthly military history magazine in the English language. Since its inception, it has built up an unrivalled reputation among military historians, enthusiasts, collectors, re-enactors, and military modellers for authoritative articles, primary research, rare photographs, and specially commissioned artwork spanning the entire history of warfare from ancient to modern – including the most popular periods such as World Wars Two and One, Napoleonic Wars, and ancient and medieval combat.

Copies of the magazine are available on newsstands and in specialist shops or can be obtained directly from the publisher on subscription from:

Military Illustrated
45 Willowhayne Avenue
East Preston
West Sussex
BN16 1PL
Great Britain
Tel: 01903 775121

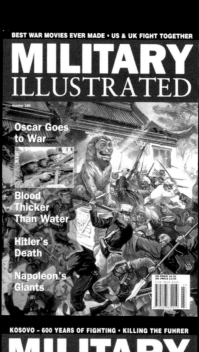

BIBLIOGRAPHY

Books

Campbell, Bert L & Ron Reynolds.,
Marine Badges & Insignia of the World,
Dorset: Blandford Press, 1983.
Canfield, Bruce N., *Complete Guide
to the M1 Garand and the M1 Carbine,*
Lincoln: RI, 1998.
Clifford, Kenneth J., *Progress and Purpose:
A Developmental History of the U.S. Marine
Corps 1900-1970,* Washington, D.C.:
History and Museums Division,
Headquarters, USMC, 1973.
Cureton, Charles H., *The U.S. Marine Corps,*
London: Greenhill Books, 1997.
Donnelly, Ralph W., *The Confederate States
Marine Corps: The Rebel Leathernecks,*
Shippensburg, Pennsylvania: The White
Mane Publishing Company, Inc., 1989.
Ellis, John, *The Sharp End: The Fighting
Man in World War II,* Pimlico: London, 1993.
Gander, Terry J., *The Bazooka: Hand-held
Hollow-charge Anti-tank Weapons,* London:
PRC Publishing Ltd., 1998.
Griffith, II, Samuel, *The Battle
of Guadalcanal,* Philadelphia:
J. P. Lippincott Co., 1963.
Hatch, Gardner N., & William Banning (eds.),
*Heritage Years: Second Marine Division
Commemorative Anthology, 1940-1949,*
Paducah, Kentucky: Turner Publishing
Company, 1988.
Heinl, Jr., Robert Debs, *Soldiers of the Sea:
The United States Marine Corps, 1775-
1962,* Annapolis: United States Naval
Insitute, 1962.
Lawliss, Chuck, *The Marine Book:
A Portrait of America's Military Elite,*
New York: Thames and Hudson, 1988.
Letcher, Brigadier General John S. Letcher,
USMC (ret.), *One Marine's Story,*
Verona, Virginia: McClure Press, 1970.
Lewis, Kenneth, *Doughboy to GI:
US Army Clothing and Equipment
1900-1945,* West Midlands:
Norman D. Landing Publishing, 1993.
Manchester, William, *Goodbye,
Darkness: a Memoir of the Pacific War,*
Boston: Little Brown, 1980.

McClellan, Major Edwin North,
*Uniforms of the American Marines,
1775 to 1829,* Washington, D.C.:
History and Museums Division,
Headquarters, U.S. Marine Corps, 1974.
McMillan, George, *The Old Breed: A History
of the First Marine Division in World War II,*
New York: Infantry Journal Press, 1949.
Moran, Jim, *U.S. Marine Corps Uniforms
& Equipment in World War 2,*
London: Windrow & Greene, 1992.
Moskin, J. Robert, *The Story of the
U.S. Marine Corps,* New York:
Paddington Press Ltd., 1979.
Millett, Allan R., *Semper Fidelis – The History
of the United States Marine Corps,* New York:
MacMillan Publishing Co., Inc., 1980.
Polmar, Norman & Peter B. Mersky,
Amphibious Warfare: An Illustrated History,
London: Blandford Press, 1988.
Parker, William D., *A Concise History of the
United States Marine Corps 1775-1969,*
Washington, D.C.: Historical Division,
Headquarters, USMC, 1970.
Proehl, Carl W., *The Fourth Marine
Division in World War II,* Washington:
Infantry Journal Press, 1946.
Richardson, W., *The Epic of Tarawa,*
London: Odhams Press Ltd., n.d.
Rottman, Gordon, & Mike Chappel,
US Marine Corps 1941–45, London:
Osprey, 1995.
Shaw, Henry I., *Tarawa: a legend is born,*
London: Purnell's History of the Second
World War, 1968.
Siefring, Thomas A., *United States Marines,*
London: Bison Books Ltd., 1979.
Simmons, Brigadier General Edwin H.,
The United States Marines, London:
Leo Cooper Ltd., 1974.
Sledge, Eugene, *With the Old Breed
at Peleliu and Okinawa',* California:
Presidio Press, 1981.
Smith, Charles Richard, *A Pictorial History:
The Marines in the Revolution,* Washington,
D.C.: History and Museums Division,
Headquarters, U.S. Marine Corps;
U.S. Government Printing Office, 1975.
Smith, W.H.B., *Small Arms of the World,*
London: Arms & Armour Press, 1973.

Sullivan, David M., *The United States
Marine Corps in the Civil War – The First
Year,* Shippensburg, Pennsylvania: The White
Mane Publishing Company, Inc., 1997.

Primary sources and articles

Brown, Major L.A., *The Marine's Handbook,*
Maryland: The United States Naval Institute,
1940.
Conley, Loy, & Richard Ugino,
'Marine Paratroopers, 1940-1945', Military
Collector & Historian, Vol. XLVII, No. 4
(Winter 1995), Washington, D.C.:
Company of Military Historians.
Conley, Loy, & Richard Ugino, 'Marine
Raider Battalions, 1942-1944',
Military Collector & Historian, Vol. XLVI,
No. 1 (Spring 1994), Washington, D.C.:
Company of Military Historians.
Freeborn, Dallas W., *The Development
of the M-1 Helmet Liner,* Military Collector
& Historian, Vol. XLIII, No. 4 (Winter 1991),
Washington, D.C.: Company of Military
Historians.
Magruder, Lt. Col. John H., 'U.S. Marine
Corps, 1797-1804', Military Collector
& Historian, Washington, D.C.:
Company of Military Historians, 1956.
McBarron, Jr., H. Charles, 'Captain Robert
Mullan's Company, Continental Marines,
1779', Military Collector & Historian,
Washington, D.C.: Company of Military
Historians, 1949.
Shaw, Henry I. et al, 'History of U.S. Marine
Corps Operations in World War II', vol. 3,
Central Pacific Drive, Washington:
Historical Branch, HQMC, 1966.
Smith-Christmas, Kenneth L.,
*The Marine Corps Utility Uniforms of World
War II,* Military Collector & Historian, Vol.
XLIII, No. 4 (Winter 1991), Washington, D.C.:
Company of Military Historians.
'Uniform Regulations, United States Marine
Corps, 1929, with plates', U.S. Government
Printing Office, Washington, 1930.
'Uniform Regulations, United States Marine
Corps, 1937', U.S. Government Printing
Office, Washington, 1937.

MARINE DIRECTORY

Museums

**Marine Corps Historical
Center and Museum**

Washington Navy Yard, Washington, D.C.
20374—0580, USA. Phone: 202 433 4882
Fax: 202 433 8200.
The Marine Corps Museum houses a
standing exhibit which details the history
of the Marine Corps from 1775 to the
present. Uniforms, small arms, medals,
accoutrements, art, photographs, and
documents are combined in a 'time tunnel'
which covers the last 200-plus years of
Marine Corps history in 20 different
chronological displays. Other resources of
the Historical Center, including personal
papers and art collections, library, and
archives, are available to researchers by
appointment, phone: 202 433 3840.

**United States Marine Corps
Air/Ground Museum**

Brown Field, Quantico, Virginia, 22134, USA.
Phone: 703 784 2606.
Housed in 1920s hangars at the Marine
Corps Combat Development Command,
the Air-Ground Museum gives visitors a
glimpse of Marine Corps air-ground team
development and its achievements in two
major wars plus numerous minor campaigns.
The buildings which house the museum are
themselves historic structures, being
examples of early aircraft hangars.
The interiors have been modified for the
exhibit of historic aircraft and ground
weapons, and illustrates the development
of doctrine, tactics, and technology.

US Marine Raider Museum

1142 W. Grace Street, Richmond, Virginia.
Phone: 804 353 1812.
Contains weapons, uniforms, photographs
and other artifacts.

**Command Museum of the Marine
Corps Recruit Depot**

1600 Henderson Ave., No. 212, San Diego,
CA 92140, USA. Phone: 619 524 6038.
On the same grounds where more than half
of all U.S. Marines endure 'boot' camp, the
depot traces the Corps' 200 years of warfare
and weaponry. Exhibits are built around the
theme 'First to Fight' and showcase
weapons, uniforms, combat writings, photos,
plus the paintings by Charles Waterhouse,
USMC Retired.

Civil Engineer Corps/SeeBee Museum

Naval Construction Battalion Center,
Port Hueneme, CA 93043-5000, USA.
Phone: 805 982 5163.

Collections and Organisations

**Records of the United States
Marine Corps**

Record Group 127, National Archives
and Records Administration, Washington,
D.C. 20408, USA.
Contains service records; correspondence,
issuances, and other records of the Office of
the Commandant, 1798—1939; maps and
photographs.

**United States Marine Corps
Research Center**

Marine Corps Base Quantico, Virginia.
Library contains the single largest collection
of private papers of officers and enlisted
men. Collections also emphasize amphibious
warfare, military science, and related
subjects. Archives collects and preserves
books, papers, maps, photographs, visual
media materials, or other documentary
sources, regardless of physical form or
characteristics, made or received by the
University and Marine Corps at large.

**The Anne S. K. Brown Military
Collection** at Brown University holds the
collection of Marine Corps war artist Harry
Daniels Reeks. Contact Peter Harrington,
Curator, Anne S.K. Brown Military Collection,
Box A, Brown University Library, Providence,
RI 02912, USA. Phone: 401 863 2414,
Fax: 401 863 2093.

The Company of Military Historians
has published many articles on the uniforms
and history of the U.S. Marine Corps in its
quarterly journal, *Military Collector &
Historian*. This society has also produced
numerous colour plates on the subject
in its series 'Military Uniforms in America'.
For details on membership write to
The Company of Military Historians,
North Main Street, Connecticut 06498, U.S.A.

National Headquarters

Marine Corps League, P.O. Box 3070,
Merrifield, VA 22116, USA.
Phone 800 625 1775 or 703 207 9588;
Fax: 703 207 0047.
This organisation offers a goldmine of
information regarding the USMC present
and past.

Memorials

U.S. Marine Corps Memorial,
Arlington National Cemetery, Virginia.
This 78-foot memorial commemorates all the
Marines who have died in battle since 1775.

USS Arizona Memorial,
Pearl Harbor, Hawaii, USA.
The final resting place for 1,102 crewmen,
including 109 Marines, of the USS Arizona
who lost their lives on December 7, 1941.
They are still entombed within the Arizona
herself. The sunken battleship is
commemorated by a 184 foot-long floating
memorial structure, designed by Alfred Preis,
that spans its mid-portion. There are three
sections in the memorial: the entry and
assembly rooms, a central or middle area,
used for observations of the sunken ship and
for ceremonies. The third section is the
shrine room. The room contains the names
of all those killed on the Arizona and their
names are engraved on a marble wall. In
recent years, the memorial has come to
represent all the military and associated
personnel killed at Pearl Harbor.

Midway Island, in the Pacific, is a treasure trove for history buffs, as the atoll still carries many historic remnants of the Battle of Midway. Although a majority of the battle took place at sea, gun emplacements, bunkers, and memorials commemorate the valiant soldiers who fought the famous battle. In May 1987, several ammunition magazines, a pillbox, and two gun emplacements on the west side of Sand Island were designated as National Historic Landmarks and listed on the National Register of Historic Places. An additional 55 sites are considered eligible for the National Register and will be reused, secured, or otherwise protected, including marine barracks, seaplane hangar and ramps, torpedo shops, radar buildings, gun emplacements, pillboxes, and Eastern Island runways.

American Memorial Park

PO Box 5198, Saipan, MP 96950, Northern Mariana Islands.
Phone: 670 234 7207 Fax: 670 234 6698.
A 'living memorial' to honor those who died in the Marianas Campaign of World War II, consisting of 133 acres of developed memorial, recreational facilities and undeveloped wetlands.

War in the Pacific National Historical Park

P.O. Box FA, Agana, Guam 96910.
Phone: 671-477-9362 or 472-7240;
Fax: 671-472-7241.
Includes major historic sites associated with the 1944 battle for Guam, an example of the island-hopping military campaign against the Japanese. The park contains seven distinct units illustrating various aspects of the struggle. Ageing gun emplacements and other military equipment relics also can be seen. Warning: live ordnance may still be found throughout the park. Some open caves may still contain booby traps.

Beirut Military Memorial Site

Arlington National Cemetery, Virginia.
Dedicated to the US servicemen, including 272 Marines, whose lives were stolen in the Beirut bombing, October 23, 1983. A Cedar Tree of Lebanon grows in living memory of those killed in the Beirut terrorist attack and all victims of terrorism around the world.

Living History, Re-enactors, and Suppliers

Military History Education Company

7742 New Providence Drive,
No 103 Falls Church, VA 22042, USA.
Phone: 703 573 0757
e-mail: marketeer@earthlink.net.
MHEC specialise in 20th Century military history re-enactments, including in US

Marine Corps, US Army Airborne, and SpecOps. In addition to producing re-enactments, MHEC also offers itself as a resource to the filming industry and the modern day military.

World War Two Impressions

7165 Adwen St., Downey, Ca. 90241, USA.
Phone/fax 562 927 6922.
Wide range of replica WWII US Uniforms and Accessories, including U.S. Marine Corps.

United States Marine Corps French Living History Group

Contact: Bruno De Vargas, 225 rue du Bois, 62136 Richebourg, France.
Tél/Fax : (33).3.21.25.24.07.
E-mail : usmc-flhg@wanadoo.fr
Website: membres.tripod.fr/USMC/french.html

Norman D. Landing

Dedicated to US Militaria, 1900-1945,
76 Alma Road, Winton, Bournemouth,
BH9 1AN, UK. Phone: 01202 521944.

WWI USMC re-enactment group

affiliated to Great War Association.
Contact Richard Roberts,
1208 South 4th St., Stoughton,
WI 53589, USA.

Arizona Historical Association

Contact Jeff Young, P.O. Box 41644,
Dept. r.N., Mesa, AZ 85274-1644, USA.

Echelon is a newsletter aimed at the WW2 re-enactor. E-mail: Echelon39@aol.com.

Internet

Headquarters, United States Marine Corps www.hqmc.usmc.mil

Marine Link www.usmc.mil

Contains information for & about Marines; current news & video; Marines Magazine; history; career information; public events; The Commandant's Page; histories of Marine Expeditionary Units.

United States Marine Corps Air/Ground Museum

aeroweb.brooklyn.cuny.edu/museums/va/usmcagm.htm
Contains description of museum facilities, plus aircraft reference data.

United States Marine Corps Research Center www.mcu.quantico.

usmc.mil /www/mcrc.htm.
Contains access to many research facilities.

Marine Corps Times

www.va2.enews.com/magazine/
0,1019,1203,00.html.cmd
Contains an electronic Newsstand & Chatroom.

USMC Living History Unit

www.mhea-hq.org/equipment.html
A Division of the Military History Education Association.

United States Marine Corps

members.tripod.com/~TheMarines/index.html
Contains a history of the Corps, current information, plus an image gallery.

Marine Corps Recruit Depot

www.cpp.usmc.mil/MCRD.NSF
Contains a history of the Marine Corps Recruit Depot, 1911-1974; picture essay on the Marines in the Boxer Rebellion 1900; picture essay on the Fourth Marines in China, 1927-1941; index of Pictures from the Depot and its Museum.

The World Wide Virtual Library

www.iit.edu/~vlnavmar/marines.html
Provides numerous listings of USMC related sites.

Memorials and Casualty Lists

members.tripod.com/~rosters/index-17.html
Contains data on Memorial Day, Pearl Harbor, Korean War, Vietnam Veterans' Memorial Wall, Beirut Memorial, plus search page & POW-MIA database.

American Memorial Park

Saipan, Northern Mariana Islands
www.nationalparks.org/guide/parks/american-mem-1993.htm

War in the Pacific National Historical Park www.nps.gov/wapa/

Vietnam Veterans Memorial Wall Page

thewall-usa.com/index.html
Contains Photo Gallery, Mailing list, Message Center, Electronic rubbings, literary works.

Civil War Marines

civilwarmarines.co./reviews.html
Contains reviews and order form for David M. Sullivan's monumental series of books on the USMC during the Civil War years.

INDEX

ACKNOWLEDGEMENTS

The author would like to thank the following, without whose help this study would not have been possible: Danny J. Crawford, Head, Reference Section, & Jack Dyer, Head of the Art Unit, History and Museums Division, Headquarters United States Marine Corps, Washington, D.C.; Kenneth L. Smith-Christmas, Curator, USMC Air-Ground Museum, Quantico; David M. Sullivan; Colonel Charles Waterhouse, USMCR (Ret); John A. Stacey; Peter Harrington, Curator, Anne S. K. Brown Military Collection, Brown University; Michael Winey, Curator of Photography, United States Army Military History Institute, Carlisle, Pennsylvania; Andrea Bankoff, Deputy Director, The Granger Collection, New York; Ian Carter, Photograph Archivist, Imperial War Museum, London; Herb Woodend, Curator, & Richard Jones, Assistant Custodian, Ministry of Defence Pattern Room, Nottingham; Bill Koplitz, US Naval Institute, Photo Service, Annapolis, Maryland; James Enos; Dr. William Schultz; Peter Newark; Alan Thrower; Ed Milligan; Andrew H. Lipps; Jean S. and Frederic A. Sharf; Donna Eitner, King Visual Technology, Inc, Maryland; Rhea Bowen, Photo Communications, Inc.; Andrea Jones and the Bibliographic Services Team, Gloucestershire County Library; Elizabeth Lal, Library Manager, Stow-on-the-Wold Library, Gloucester Library Services; David Durston; Kurt Hughes; Ken Lewis; Norman Stahl and Joseph H. Alexander, and Lou Reda Productions Inc., for permission to quote from 'Iwo Jima: Hell's Volcano' and 'Okinawa: The Final Battle'; and a special thanks to Gardner N. Hatch, Publisher's Editor, Turner Publishing Company, Paducah, Kentucky, & William Banning, Editor, Second Marine Division Association, for permission to quote from the memoirs of so many Marines published in *Heritage Years: Second Marine Division Commemorative Anthology, 1940–1949*, and to Jim Moran for generously sharing his collection, knowledge, and wisdom regarding the history and uniforms of the Marine Corps.

Semper Fidelis!